THE BOUNDING SPRING

A HISTORY OF TEFFONT IN WILTSHIRE

Tef—old Frisian for boundary
Fontana—Latin for spring

In memory of Joan Willan,
who was the inspiration for this book

THE BOUNDING SPRING

A HISTORY OF TEFFONT IN WILTSHIRE

AUDREY McBAIN AND LYNETTE NELSON

First published in the United Kingdom in 2003 by
Black Horse Books

ISBN 1-904377-26-2

British Library Cataloguing in Publication Data
The Bounding Spring - A History of Teffont in Wiltshire
Audrey McBain and Lynette Nelson

Black Horse Books
Frith's Barn, Teffont,
Salisbury, Wiltshire SP3 5QP
Tel: +44 (0) 1722 716 376

Project Editor: Emma Johnston-Brown
Designed and assembled: Terence Sackett
Images scanned: Heather Crisp

Printed and bound in Great Britain

Jacket photographs by Victoria Knowles

Teffont Magna in the 19th century.

Teffont Evias in the 19th century.

CONTENTS

1	FROM HORSETAILS TO OX-PLOUGHS	6
2	ROMAN INTERLUDE	18
3	A GLIMPSE INTO THE DARK AGES	22
4	GOOD DAYS, BAD DAYS AND DOMESDAY	27
5	FROM BLACK DEATH TO CLOTH OF GOLD	35
6	TIP-TOEING THROUGH THE TUDORS	42
7	CIVIL WAR AND JOYLESS PEACE	50
8	FROM ASHES TO ASHES	59
9	NEW LANDLORDS AND A NEW ROAD	64
10	MAINLY THE MAYNES	73
11	THE RICH MAN IN HIS CASTLE, THE POOR MAN AT HIS GATE	85
12	WAR AND PEACE	96
13	THE STREAM	113
	INDEX	135

CHAPTER ONE

FROM HORSETAILS TO OX-PLOUGHS

This book has been written to celebrate the beginning of the third millennium in Teffont, a small village with a long and varied history, situated in a valley which has sustained human life for considerably more than two millennia.

To enter Teffont from the north, into Teffont Magna, is to see a typical chalkland village set in softly rolling downs dissected by dry valleys, and a stream flowing alongside the road. To enter from the south, into Teffont Evias, is to see a rougher terrain, with large rocks jutting from the sides of the valley, but with the same stream continuing to edge the road. The difference is a result of the adventurous physical history of the village, which took place in several stages over millions of years (for reference purposes there is a geological time chart on page 135).

Jurassic or Cretaceous ammonite found at Manor Farm, Teffont Magna. (VK)

The earliest rocks in Wiltshire were laid down in the Devonian period, which started about 395 million years ago. Wiltshire was under the sea for much of this period. But even when the sea receded, the area as it is today would have been unrecognisable. The valley, stream, downs and rocks were not to be in place for millions of years. The only living things would have been the first amphibians hauling themselves on to the land, where the first plants were beginning to emerge, among them the horsetail—or 'scouring-rush'—which still makes an unwelcome appearance in our gardens. The area was not even in its present latitude; it was below the equator, landlocked in a huge continent, and the climate was hot.

During the 150 million years following this period, the area would undergo many changes. Firstly there was the warm and wet time of the Carboniferous period, with its forests of 100-foot-high tree ferns, giant horsetails and club mosses, which harboured dragonflies with a two-foot wing span and scorpions three feet long. During the following Permian and Triassic periods, the land was transformed into a hot dry desert. There may have been a mountain range to the north of the Teffont area, or even over it, but this eroded to low hills, bare of vegetation, on which lizards and other reptiles basked.

Jurassic echinoid found in a Teffont Magna garden. (EF)

There were many periods of interest during the following millennia. The first known stone to be formed, Portland stone, is buried beneath the whole village, but a small earth movement brought it to the surface in the Chilmark ravine on the western boundary, enabling it eventually to be mined and used for many important buildings, including Salisbury Cathedral, as well as the church at Teffont Evias.

Portland stone belongs to the Jurassic period, when a variety of exotic creatures would have swum over the village area, including ichthyosaurs, giant pliosaurs, sharks and rays, while ammonites the size of lorry wheels floated on the surface. Later in this period the seas retreated for over 20 million years, apart from brief encroachments; one of these left the notable cinder bed, full of oyster shells. But Teffont was still under water in a fresh-water lake at times. This was when the Purbeck stone was laid down; this stone lies buried beneath the chalk in Teffont Magna, but it is prominent in Teffont Evias, and has been quarried for centuries past for use in humbler projects than those in which Portland stone was used, such as local cottages and bridges and more recently for the production of lime.

This account of our geological history is not mere conjecture. There is the evidence of numerous fossils, most of which have been recovered from the Teffont and Chilmark quarries, as well as fossilized sea shells occasionally found in village gardens. In 1893 the Reverend W H Andrews and A Jukes-Browne excavated to seven feet below the Teffont quarry floor on Butts Hill, and drew up a schedule of plants and animal parts fossilized in the limestone. These include conifers, crocodiles, turtles, sharks, ichthyosaurs, various fish, oysters, mussels, ammonites, clam-shrimps, belemnites, sea urchins, ostracods, bivalves, beetles and dragon-flies.

In 1838 another enterprising clergyman, the Reverend Peter Brodie, discovered a range of insect fossils of the late Jurassic in Purbeck stone at a quarry site near Teffont (the fossils are now in the Natural History Museum, London). Their sharp definition indicates that they were covered quickly, suggesting a sudden change of weather or a natural calamity. The wide variety of species, including bugs, beetles, roaches, wasps, hoppers, caddis and dragon-flies, affords a glimpse into the environment in which they lived: a land with fresh water, where forests of cycads and conifers (and later oaks and magnolias, perhaps) gave shade. The insects are of a primitive type and mainly extinct, but they are not dissimilar to the ones we see today.

The early years of the chalk or Cretaceous period, starting 140 million years ago, were relatively uneventful. The Wealden stone was formed when Teffont was either in a giant delta draining a great river from the west, or beneath a lake. Then it was covered first by a shallow sea, which left the Lower

Greensand stone, secondly by an extremely deep sea, which laid a layer of clay, or gault, and finally by another shallower one which formed the Upper Greensand. These rocks have weathered down to a good fertile loam, and those with gardens on it are the envy of their neighbours on the hungry chalk.

The chalk, so noticeable in Magna but absent in Evias, was the last layer of stone to be laid down. It was formed as a result of one of the greatest inundations of Britain and Europe, which began about 90 million years ago. The land was flooded with clear, warm water deeper than the height of several Salisbury Cathedrals. Over more than 20 million years, 200-300 metres of chalk built up, formed when the shells and skeletons of countless plants and animals settled on the sea bed and formed a soft white limestone. When the land rose above the sea over 65 million years ago, there would have been a gently sloping plain of chalk over Teffont as far as the eye could see.

The flints which are still found everywhere in parts of Teffont were formed later when the land was above the sea. The spines of creatures such as sponges, which had been suspended in the chalk, were dissolved by rainwater, and the resulting silica gel filled cavities left in the chalk by worm burrows and empty shells. Millions of years later these would provide early man with material for his hunting weapons. The hunter, however, was not even a twinkle in a dinosaur's eye when the Tertiary Age began 65 million years ago. On the other hand, the animals he would hunt were just over the horizon, for the giant reptilians disappeared, leaving the mammals to take over the earth.

The next major development in the physical history of the village took place when an earlier earth fault was reactivated. Its core was over Teffont Evias, and the earth's crust over the area was pushed up into a fold. In the upheaval the Purbeck rocks were thrown up to the surface from beyond Tisbury, through Teffont Evias and on to Barford. A crack opened up along the crest of the fold; weathering and erosion eventually turned it into the bed of the River Nadder. Over millions of years the sides of the valley eroded to a gentle slope, and the fold became a valley. In Teffont the remnant of the fold can be seen where the wooded Greensand ridge edges the old Dinton Road.

Jurassic fish fossils from Purbeck beds in a Teffont Evias quarry. (VK)

The fault and the subsequent erosion of the valley side have provided a richly varied geology, with representatives of all the formations between Portland stone and the Upper Chalk exposed within the length of the village.

This rock formation eventually led to the creation of a spring line, allowing the water to come to the surface between the bands of impenetrable clay and Upper Greensand, forming the stream which runs through the village.

The basic foundations of the valley were in place, but the landscape continued to undergo further modifications. Even during the last 700,000 years, monumental changes have occurred. This was the tail end of the 2 million-year-long Pleistocene period, or Ice Age. The term Ice Age is misleading. Although for thousands of years the land was indeed in the grip of permafrost, there were also interglacial periods, when the temperature swung to sub-tropical levels. These swings brought about what was almost the final form of the chalkland terrain.

Late Jurassic insect fossil: obliogaster fittoni ('True Fly') found by Brodie near Teffont Evias Quarry. *Courtesy of The Wiltshire Archaeological Society*

At the end of each cold period, when the ground thawed, the melt-off produced vigorous streams, strong enough to carry boulders and to cut into the chalk to form deep valleys. Massive amounts of water were produced, so that the area would have been repeatedly flooded; the water eventually drained into the Nadder, and from there into an ancient river system, eventually reaching the sea.

The vegetation varied according to the climate; the warmer it became, the denser the vegetation, and the type of vegetation influenced the species of animals arriving from Europe, to which Britain was still attached.

Only the hardiest animals would have ventured into the Teffont area when the glacials were at their coldest. However, it is known that during some of the brief Arctic summers, woolly mammoths, reindeer and woolly rhinoceros were present locally, feeding on sedges, mosses and artemisias. When the decreasing cold permitted the growth of grass, they would be joined by herbivores, notably bison and wild horses, who in turn were followed by the carnivores: cave lions, bears, wolves and cave hyenas. Bones of most of these animals have been found in the Salisbury area, as well as those of lemmings, arctic geese and arctic foxes.

As the temperature continued to rise, woodland would have taken over, attracting different fauna, ranging from woodland elephants, rhinoceros and hippopotamus to deer, foxes, badgers, wolves, beavers and hedgehogs, with robins, starlings and owls inhabiting the trees. An extinct variety of water voles was also present. One creature which was definitely a local resident was a red squirrel, which left its bones nearby.

The first appearance of prehistoric man in Britain is recorded as being in about 500,000 BC. But it is not until about 250,000 BC that he is believed to have ventured into Wiltshire. These people came in small bands during temperate periods, armed with spruce staves and their multi-purpose flint hand-axes (prehistoric man's equivalent of the Swiss Army knife). They made frequent forays into the area over the next 50,000 years, chiefly in pursuit of wild pig, deer and wild oxen; they were happy also to scavenge any large beasts from the jaws of wolves or bears, if they could. The Salisbury area is rich in their tools, washed down from the surrounding valleys by torrents of water during glacial melt periods. Although no tools of this period have been found in Teffont, a hand-axe was discovered a short distance away in Stapleford.

Men and animals were driven away by another glacial beginning 200,000 years ago. The hunters who replaced them in about 75,000 BC, in the wake of large herds of cold-climate herbivores, were of a different type: the Neanderthals. One of their hand-axes was found below the bones of a mammoth in Salisbury. To the hunters of that day, who had crossed the land-bridge from Europe on foot, our valley must have seemed just a short stride away, so Neanderthal man may well have left his footsteps here.

The ancestors of modern man—homo sapiens sapiens—made a brief appearance in the locality shortly before the onset of the Devensian glacial some 34,000 years ago. That they were more sophisticated than their predecessors is testified by their use of specialized tools for different tasks and their wider use of natural resources, such as bone and mammoth ivory for certain tools. Most such artefacts have been found in distant caves, where the hunters appear to have sheltered from the cold. However, two flint tools discovered in the 20th century by the Reverend G H Engleheart and Dr G C Clay at Fir Hill, between Teffont and Fovant, may belong to this period.

Arctic conditions some time after 25,000 BC drove people away; they were not to return again until 13,500 years ago.

Over the next 3,000 years the climate fluctuated between cold and warm. Usually the changes were gradual, but around 8,300 BC the temperature surged from extreme cold to temperatures higher than those of today in the space of 50 years. The melt-down associated with this rapid thaw sent torrents of water rushing across the plains. As a result, the Nadder Valley was scoured one final time before the topography of our local landscape took its final shape. The warmer climate led to the afforestation of vast tracks of the country, which attracted different fauna: deer, auroch and wild boar replaced the herbivores of the plains. This inevitably led to the development of revolutionary hunting techniques. The people who initiated them are referred to as Mesolithic, or Middle Stone Age people. But they were much more than a link between the Old (Paleolithic) and the New Stone Age. They were skilled and innovative; they used bows and arrows, and stalked their prey through the trackless forests, sometimes using dogs to aid them. They are particularly significant in the history of Britain, since the warmer climate enabled significant numbers of them to over-winter here.

After about 6,000 BC, escaping to the southern lands was no longer an option; the swollen seas caused by the melting ice had spilt over to form the English Channel and cut Britain off from the Continent.

The Mesolithic people probably made their way through the forested landscape following the course of rivers, setting up temporary camps in places which met their needs. Many such sites are found in the Vale of Wardour. One of these was Teffont.

Evidence of Mesolithic occupation in the form of worked flints has been found at several sites around Teffont. The fact that the finds are predominantly composed of flint cores and discarded flakes suggests that they were on the sites of a flint-producing industry. Not many finished implements were found: just the odd scraper and burin (chisel), and a few of the tiny, finely made bladelets which are a hallmark of Mesolithic culture. They were used as arrow heads, or were set into a handle to make a long cutting tool. One such bladelet was identified as a 'Horsham point'. This information may not stir the emotions of our readers, but it excited the finders, since it enabled them to date the collection to the Late Mesolithic.

The consistently high quality of the Mesolithic flint production suggests that these 'knappers' were designated craftsmen within the community. It is not unreasonable to suppose that there was at least a temporary camp housing the rest of the community not far from the production site.

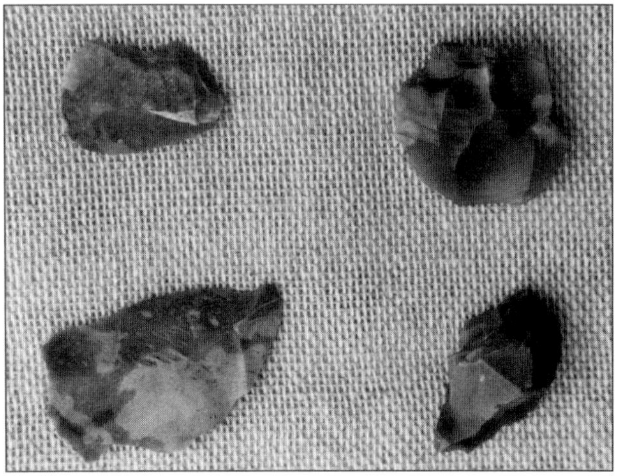
Neolithic flint scrapers found in Teffont Evias. (EF)

The area of Teffont meets the conditions which Mesolithic man customarily sought when choosing a campsite: it had to be near a chalk or greensand area, and close to a river or spring. The advantage of this soil type was that it supported a lighter woodland, mainly of oak, elm, ash, yew and alder. Such a terrain made for easier hunting and access to nuts and berries than the dense forest produced by the rich clay of nearby Holt Lane and Grovely Wood, for instance. The latter, however, would have provided a source of flints, another essential requirement for a Mesolithic settlement.

One untypical Mesolithic implement was discovered in the parish north-west of Thickthorn Copse. It is shaped like a squashed sphere, with a hole drilled through the middle. It has sometimes been described as a mace-head, but its use is uncertain. It may simply have been a cult object. It is of particular interest because it is made not of flint, but of epidiorite, a mineral whose nearest source was Cornwall.

Evidence of Mesolithic camps is rarely found, for they were constructed of bio-degradable materials; the shelters were made from animal skins suspended on wooden frames. The Mesolithic settlers were not, however, environmentally friendly in every respect. It is believed that they employed 'slash and burn' methods of forest clearance, both to promote the growth of grass, which would lure deer to come and graze, and to encourage the spread of hazel, for hazel nuts provided an important part of their diet. They left evidence of their tree-felling activities in Teffont in the form of a designated tool, a 'tranchet axe', which is a flint axe set at right-angles in a wooden handle. Thus, although the Mesolithic people did not undertake any real agriculture, they took a large step in that direction. Even though this degree of forest clearance would have made little impact at the time, they must be held responsible for initiating the process of deforestation which was to change our landscape so drastically.

Around the middle of the 5th millennium BC, new people made their appearance in Wessex who were to revolutionise completely the way of life in Britain; some of them subsequently settled in Teffont. They are known as the Neolithic, or New Stone Age people. Their origin is a matter of controversy. Some experts claim that they were new immigrants from Europe; others maintain that they were descendants of the resident Mesolithic.

Neolithic polished flint axe. (EF)

Their life-style, however, most certainly came from Europe. There the practice of farming livestock and growing crops had gradually spread north from the Middle East. By one means or another it was introduced into Britain. Initially it was dominated by cattle- and pig-breeding. Whether the stock was the result of domesticating the local aurochs and wild pigs or whether the progenitors at least were brought across the Channel is another matter of controversy. The sheep or goats which eventually followed, and the original seeds of barley, einkorn and emmer wheat, would have been imported, since they were not available within the island. An ard (a simple wooden plough) found at Avebury is evidence of agriculture in the area.

The change, however, from being hunter-gatherers to food-growing communities was a gradual one. Although many Neolithic artefacts have been found on Salisbury Plain, the almost total absence of traces of domestic habitation suggests that the people maintained a semi-nomadic existence, frequently moving on in search of fresh pasture and more fertile ground. There would have been a layer of rich, light soil above the chalk, but without proper husbandry, it would have quickly deteriorated, obliging the farmers to clear new areas of forest. In this activity they may have had an unexpected ally in the form of the elm beetle, which is thought to have devastated the elm forest in the 4th millennium BC. The chalkland was apparently almost totally cleared by 3,500 BC, allowing the establishment of pasture and the introduction of sheep.

The most dramatic change which the Neolithic age brought about was the rise of communities sufficiently cohesive to build monuments and establish territories. The territory around Stonehenge developed into one of the most important prehistoric sites in Europe; this territory includes the Nadder Valley.

There is abundant evidence of Neolithic occupation in the area of Teffont. A large number of worked flints has been picked up from the surface of the fields. A significant number of cores, waste flakes and hammer-stones indicates the existence of a Neolithic flint industry at Ley Farm on the site of an earlier Mesolithic one. It is interesting that much of the flint had been imported, some from Chilmark, and some from Sussex and Kent. Tools fashioned from chert from Portland Bill were also found.

Distinguishing early Neolithic from Mesolithic tools requires expertise. As a general rule, it may be said that Neolithic tools are less dainty than Mesolithic ones, perhaps reflecting the fact that the Neolithic peoples led a more static life and therefore placed utility above portability when producing their tools. Later Neolithic tools are squatter and chunkier than the early ones, emphasizing the increasing trend towards settlement. The presence of tools characteristic of the different periods indicates that the Ley Farm site was continuously or recurrently in use.

The majority of the implements are late Neolithic scrapers (used especially for cleaning hides). Some have finely serrated edges, indicating considerable skill on the part of the craftsmen. Gloss along the worked edges on some tools indicates that they were used for cutting plant material. In addition, there are scrapers with semi-circular notches cut into them, probably designed to strip bark off twigs—a feature not previously recorded. Pot-boilers and grinding stones (querns) also found on the site strongly suggest the existence of domestic settlement.

Isolated implements have been found in and around the village. Among them are two polished axe-heads emanating from the Lake District, and one dolorite axe, probably from Wales. A fine example of a flint axe was dug up in Teffont Magna. Polished axes were the main items of the Neolithic tool-kit. Axes from Cumbria made from igneous rock, notably volcanic tuff, were especially popular, and were widely distributed throughout Britain (some, no doubt, passed through the Stonehenge area, since its close proximity to the River Avon would have made it an important trading centre). Polished axes could also have symbolic significance, and were perhaps offered to a neighbour as a pledge of friendship or as a tribute. Occasionally they were fashioned from jadeite (probably from Switzerland), in which case their use was ceremonial. Although no such axe has been found in the village, we have two small cushion-shaped objects made from jadeite. Their function or symbolism is unknown, but it is likely that they were cult objects of some value. An early Neolithic leaf-shaped arrow head found in the vicinity suggests that the Neolithic hunter, like his Mesolithic predecessor, was still wielding a bow in the surrounding forest.

The hunter may from time to time have been forced to exchange his bow for a red deer antler pick and an ox-shoulder shovel to assist in the great work of constructing the long barrows which were being built as tombs for the prestigious families of the community. Some of these barrows still remain as landmarks in the vicinity of Stonehenge.

There would have been no such burial for the hunter when his short life came to an end. His remains would probably have been left outside to decompose, and his bones would have been subsequently thrown into a ditch.

By the second half of the fourth millennium, however, even the most powerful families appear to have been losing their right to a barrow burial. Although the barrows were becoming ever larger and longer, they might house only one corpse, or none at all. They had, it seems, become memorials rather than tombs. It is tempting to regard them as white elephants—especially since they were originally topped with a layer of white chalk. But they may well have served as territorial markers, designed to display the power of the community and to discourage intruders.

There are indications of agricultural depression in the area and a decline in population from about 3,300 BC; this was probably caused by over-exploitation of the land, coupled with periods of heavy rainfall. However, the situation had improved sufficiently by around 2,950 BC for labour to be available to build the first circular earthwork enclosure of Stonehenge.

From about 3,000 BC the landscape around the site of Stonehenge began to change. A rash of new barrows appeared, but they were circular in shape instead of rectangular. Whether this was the result of a change of population or a change of thought is still under discussion.

Formerly it was the practice to refer to the builders of the earliest round barrows as 'Beaker People', because of the distinctive pottery they produced which was the hallmark of their culture. They made an alcoholic drink, a type of mead, from cereal and honey, and had the endearing custom of placing a beaker of it beside a corpse when they buried him. Remnants of it have been found in beakers recovered from their burial mounds. These unobtrusive early barrows were often hidden in woodland, away from the main monuments. There are early references to several such barrows in the area of Teffont, but only one, close to Grovely Wood, has survived. Sad to say, it yielded neither bones nor beaker. Fragments of beakers have, however, been found.

The nearest place to Teffont where a complete beaker has been unearthed is Berwick St James. But the Beaker People left other evidence of their presence in our parish. Certain characteristic tools, such

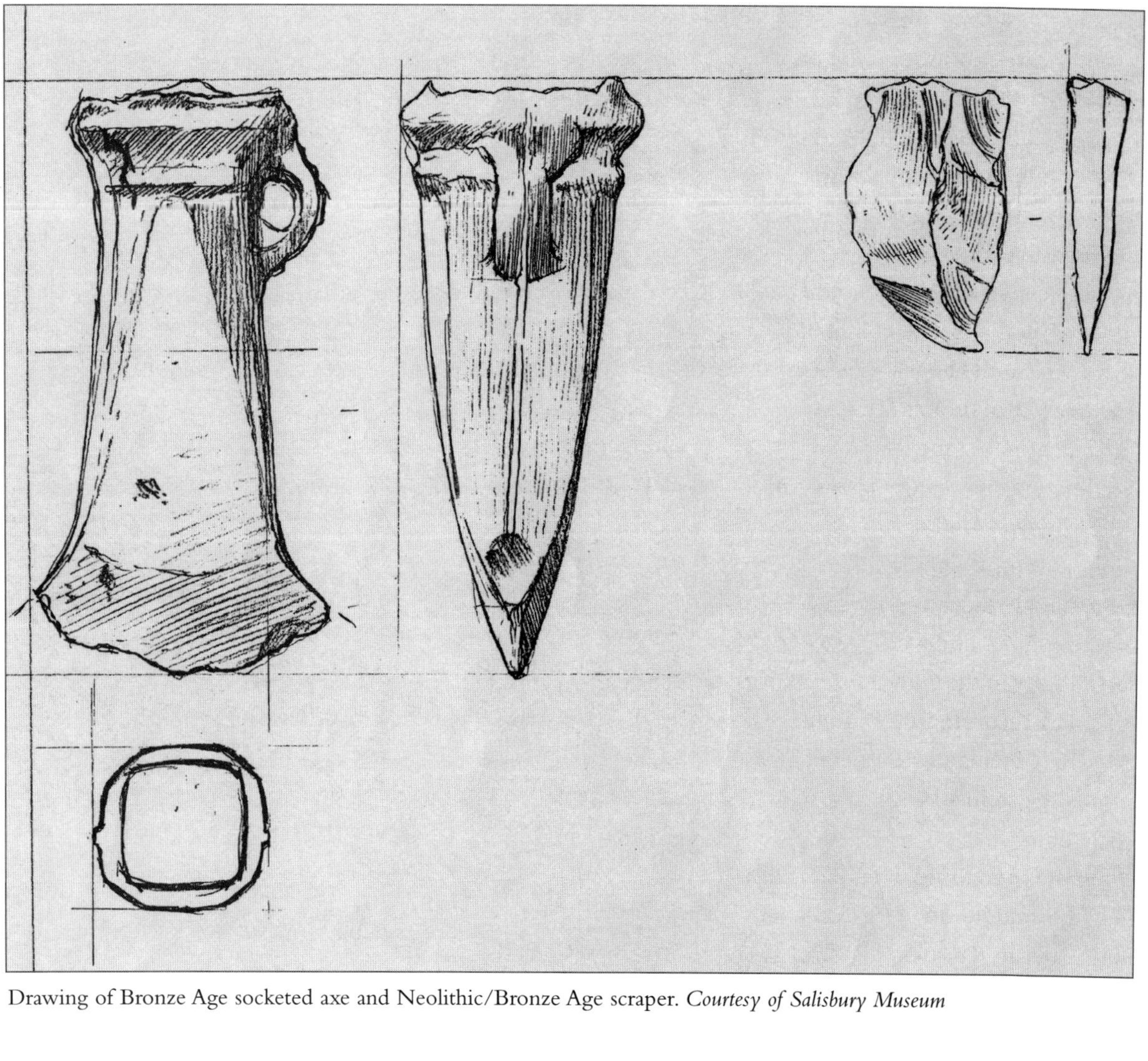

Drawing of Bronze Age socketed axe and Neolithic/Bronze Age scraper. *Courtesy of Salisbury Museum*

as tiny flint scrapers known as 'thumbnail scrapers', have been found in plenty in and around the village; tanged and barbed flint arrowheads have been picked up on surrounding farmland; and a greenstone shaft-hole adze (also typical) was discovered nearby.

Bronze Age beaker

The most celebrated beaker burial was discovered by accident quite recently, 2 miles south east of Stonehenge. Although the man within was dubbed 'the Amesbury Archer', the unprecedented richness of the tomb indicated that he was no mere bowman. Although the grave-goods included a number of arrow-heads, there were also costly imported copper artefacts and a pair of gold earrings, along with several beakers. What makes him relevant to our history is that he is deemed to have been a man of extremely high rank, possibly with dominion over a wide territory and perhaps responsible for the second-phase building at Stonehenge.

It was certainly around the time of the Amesbury Archer that building was resumed at Stonehenge (between 2,400 and 2,200 BC). The blue stones from the Preseli Mountains were erected in a circle, but they were later rearranged, and the great sarsens dragged from the Marlborough Downs were installed around them. It is estimated that this final building phase required 1,750,000 man-hours to complete. Since they were living within the territory of Stonehenge, it is unlikely that men from the Teffont area were able to escape involvement in the labour. Moreover, some of the 'packing stones' around the bases of the sarsens have been identified as coming from the Teffont/Chilmark quarries.

The period after the completion of the great monument marked the peak of the area's pre-historic eminence. Stonehenge became the focal point of the community and the dominant feature of the area. The quantity of bronze tools and weapons, in addition to rare gold items, recovered from barrows subsequently built in the vicinity indicate that this was a comparatively wealthy community with access to a wide network of trade.

Socketed axe, middle-late Bronze Age, 1400-700 BC, found in field off Holt Lane, Teffont Evias. (EF)

A few Bronze Age implements have been found in our parish. An early copper alloy socketed gouge, a bronze rapier and a dagger were picked up by R S Newall early in the 20th century, and a collection of flints was recovered from Teffont Evias quarry. In 2002, Bert Freeman discovered a fine middle/late Bronze Age copper alloy socketed axe on the edge of Holt Wood.

But the good times did not endure for long. Soon after the middle of the second millennium BC a decline began. This has sometimes been attributed to the fall of the Mycenaean Empire in the Aegean in

1400 BC, which is said to have affected trade links throughout Europe (including the lucrative export of tin from Cornwall, which perhaps passed through the Stonehenge community trade centre). Other possible reasons include a serious outbreak of plague between 1300 and 1100 BC, and the onset of a cold, wet weather phase around 1200 BC. Whatever the reason, Stonehenge fell into disuse during the 13th century BC. Trading areas and centres of wealth shifted to the east of England and the Thames Valley region, and Wessex appears to have become a cultural backwater. It did not recover until 1000-900 BC, when normal cross-Channel links to Brittany and beyond were restored, but there were to be no more elaborate burials or large barrows.

It appears that not only the monuments, but also the community disintegrated. The hill-forts which began to spring up in Wessex around this time are symptomatic of an era of insecurity.

Wick Ball Camp, which stands on the ridge between Teffont and Dinton, was probably constructed at the beginning of the first millennium. It comprises a roughly rectangular area of some nine acres, enclosed by a ditch, with ramparts 36 feet deep and a single entrance. In the absence of any excavation, it is impossible to establish either its origin or its purpose. It appears, however, to come within the category known as 'ridge end forts'; these are thought to have been the strongholds of local chieftains, and also to have been used as a meeting-place for local farmers, and a refuge for them and their herds in times of danger. The only artefact recovered from the region—a late Neolithic flint scraper—suggests that the site might have been inhabited at an earlier stage.

During the 8th century BC the region was occupied by people who, most authorities now believe, were descendants of previous inhabitants of Britain. Their life-style, however, gradually changed as a result of contact with the more advanced Celtic tribes of Europe. From them they learned the technology of iron production, which would revolutionize the lives of the farming communities.

Since iron was easier and cheaper to produce than bronze, and iron ore was more readily obtainable, it was possible for the poorer members of society to have access to it and to have tools and implements made from it. At the same time, draught animals—oxen to draw the plough and horses to pull wheeled vehicles—were introduced.

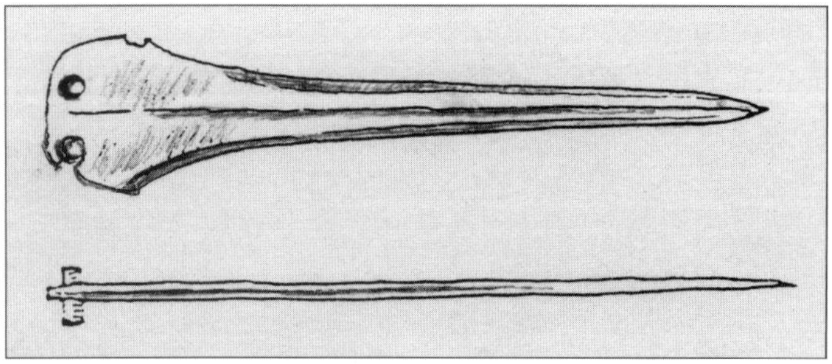

Sketch of Bronze Age rapier-shaped dagger found in Teffont by R S Newall.

Evidence of much Iron Age activity has been discovered in the Salisbury Plain area, where large hoards of tools and weapons have been found; but no more barrows were built. Iron Age man certainly showed a different attitude to the dead from his Bronze Age ancestors. He raised no tombs, and was more likely to place a heavy stone on the breast of the deceased than a beaker of mead at his elbow.

Several Iron Age villages, chiefly of the late period, have been discovered between the Nadder and the Wylye along Grovely Ridge, at sites including Hanging Langford Camp, Elsbury and—of most significance—Stockton Earthworks. Here, just a mile or so to the north-west of our parish boundary, was a flourishing settlement covering 40 hectares. Amongst a quantity of artefacts found there were spindle whorls, weaving combs and bone needles, indicating that the inhabitants raised sheep and grew flax and wore garments made from wool and linen.

The 9-mile-long Grovely 'Grims Ditch', part of which forms the Teffont parish boundary, may well have been built by these Iron Age settlers. Thousands of hectares of Wessex chalkland were encompassed by such ditches during the early Iron Age. They are believed to have constituted territorial boundaries, and within them were field systems, divided up for growing crops and grazing animals.

Iron Age people obviously visited the site of this village. One of them died here: a skeleton with a blue bead at its throat was found at the spring-head in Teffont Magna. It was described by those who found it in the 1940s as being 'hurriedly buried', but no reason was given in support of the statement. However, it was an unexpected place to find such a burial. Iron Age people regarded a spring as a place to make contact with the gods. There is the possibility that the spring had run dry, and a human sacrifice was made to placate the gods—but this is mere conjecture.

A scattering of Iron Age artefacts, including beads, polished stones and an iron spear-head, have been recovered from various parts of the village, and a coin—a silver stater—was found in Teffont Evias quarry. The latter is of especial significance, since it is an early indication that coins were being used in place of the traditional barter system. Like most Iron Age coins discovered in the area, it was of Durotrigian origin. A further silver stater was found very recently in a field north of the village. Like the previous find, it too is of Durotrigian origin, and bears a design of Apollo's head on the face and a horse on the reverse. During the latter part of the Iron Age, small tribal groups, often including Gallic immigrants, joined together to form confederations or kingdoms. Teffont appears to have been on the northern fringe of the kingdom of the Durotriges, centred in Dorset.

The Durotriges were involved in considerable cross-Channel trade, exchanging farm surpluses such as corn, wool and hides, which were needed by the Romans, for luxury items such as wine, oil, salted fish and even liquid glass. A denarius of Marcus Fannius (137-4 BC), dating from almost a century before Julius Caesar's expedition to Britain, found its way to Teffont Magna (where it was discovered more than 2000 years later) in the pocket of one of these Iron Age traders, perhaps.

During the Iron Age the natives of this country appear to have developed a culture very similar to that of their European Celtic neighbours, including their language and dress. Brooches recovered in the area suggest that they secured their cloaks by means of a brooch on the shoulder in the European Celtic style. (There was even a specialist brooch-maker in the area of Salisbury during the 4th-3rd century BC). Naturally there were variations due to the comparatively isolated situation of Britain, but the population within the island was obviously becoming more homogeneous. By the time of Julius Caesar's visit, Britain is recorded as 'having fully developed its insular Celtic character'.

CHAPTER TWO

ROMAN INTERLUDE

An inscription on the Arch of Claudius in Rome declares that he was 'first to have brought the barbarian people across the ocean under the influence of the Roman people'. The ocean in question was the English Channel, which—narrow though it was—could wreak havoc among an invading fleet, as Julius Caesar had discovered when he made his expedition to England in 55 BC.

Claudius undoubtedly gained from Caesar's experience, especially regarding the whereabouts of good harbours. Nevertheless, there was rebellion among the Roman soldiers when they learned that they were being sent to invade Britain. Despite the established trade with the island, they were terrified of crossing the 'ocean' and leaving behind the known world.

Eventually in 43 AD Claudius was able to set sail with an army of some 40,000 men, most of whom survived the crossing and landed at various points on the southern coast. The Roman legions received a mixed reception; they were welcomed by some tribes, but resisted by others. The Durotriges belonged to the latter group.

There is no evidence of any battles having taken place in this area. However, it is very possible that men from the local farms were among the warriors who vainly attempted to defend the Durotrigian forts at Hod Hill and Maiden Castle, since in times of need the professional Celtic warriors were backed up by humble levies of farmers temporarily recruited when the land could spare them. As we have already noted, the head of an iron spear, the weapon of the common foot-soldier, was unearthed in Teffont Evias.

It has been suggested that the Salisbury Plain/Cranborne Chase area was regarded by the Romans as such a hotbed of resistance that it was made an 'imperial domain' and punished by having many of its assets confiscated ; this theory has sometimes been advanced as a reason for the scarcity of villas in the area.

This seems unlikely, however, since the Grovely Ridge Iron Age settlements flourished after the invasion. Artefacts from this period discovered on the sites of the settlements show a degree of sophistication unencountered before the Roman invasion, and unexpected in a primitive agricultural community.

They include ornaments, cosmetic implements, metal spoons, coins and fragments of imported pottery and glassware. The implications are that these settlements experienced greater prosperity as well as exposure to a more sophisticated life-style, probably to a large extent the result of commerce. It is possible that they were supplying grain and hides for the Roman army.

A more likely explanation for the lack of villas is that with the whole of the country to choose from, the Romans would probably not have put our area at the top of their visiting list. Villas either developed out of prosperous farms, or were purpose-built as country estates. The chalklands were conspicuously less fertile, and the landscape, although pretty enough, was not the most scenic in southern England.

As was the case in later societies, the upper-class Romans tended to look for a little place in the Cotswolds for their country estate.

This does not preclude the possibility of a Roman presence in the area of Teffont. The name itself is very significant. The prefix may have been applied later, but 'font' is almost certainly derived from the Late Latin word for spring, 'fontana', from the Latin 'fons'. It may well be that our spring became known as a place where the traveller could be sure of finding pure water. The Romans had built a road connecting the silver and lead mines of the Mendips with Old Sarum and Winchester, passing through the north of our parish.

Evidence of Roman occupation is especially strong in the region of the Teffont and Chilmark quarries. Chilmark stone has been identified in various Roman buildings, including villas in East Grimstead and Rockbourne. The stone was very likely both mined and transported by local men under Roman supervision. Land nearby, which would later be incorporated into the Teffont/Chilmark quarry complex, apparently served as a burial ground. A large number of wooden and stone coffins have been found there. It is on record that thirty were discovered at the beginning of the 20th century, but no details of them survive. Furthermore, it is said that in the 1920s and 1930s, workers in the quarry dug up about a hundred cyst coffins (traditional British coffins fashioned from slabs of stone stuck together with clay). Information about them, however, was reportedly suppressed by the quarry authorities—no doubt they feared that if the news were to reach the ears of those nutty archaeologists, the latter might try to interfere with the important business of quarrying.

View of Holt Wood. Site of a Romano-British temple or look-out post. (VK)

The only details we have of any burials are those left by G H Engleheart concerning two graves which he discovered in the 1930s.

They comprised wooden coffins encased in stone slabs containing the much depleted remains of skeletons 'of Romano-British type', each with a collection of iron hobnails. Although hobnails in footwear were a Roman introduction, their inclusion in graves is said to derive from a native custom of providing symbolic footwear for the use of the dead in the next world, chiefly found in burials of the 3rd and 4th century in southern England.

A number of pieces of Romano-British jewellery were recovered by Sir Edgar Keatinge and Ron Lever from Teffont Evias quarry, where they had very likely been placed in coffins. One bracelet most certainly had been, since it was still attached to a fragment of humerus. Apart from a small gold torc, all the items of jewellery were bronze. The pieces most commonly found were brooches of both trumpet and disc type. One of the brooches is in the form of a horse and rider—a favourite Celtic design. (It has been suggested that the white horse at Uffington— almost certainly of Celtic origin—once bore a rider).

An arrow-head, also found at the quarry site, suggests that hunting was still taking place, but probably mainly as a sport. Dogs, including Irish wolfhounds and greyhounds, were kept for hunting (as well as being valuable export items). Their quarry included wolves, foxes, bear and deer—but not fowl or hares, which, although plentiful, were regarded as sacred by the native British.

A range of artefacts with agricultural associations was discovered around the village, indicating the vicinity of a farm. These included a large knife, a butcher's chopper, numerous potsherds, among which was a section of a perforated bowl, probably used for use in cheese-making, and the lower stone of a rotary quern. The quern, a Roman innovation, greatly facilitated the process of grinding corn.

The nearest known farm was at Eyewell, just over the Teffont/Chilmark border, which was partially excavated in 1992. It was evidently a mixed farm, for sheep and cattle bones were recovered, as well as querns and a grain dryer. The latter was an innovative device: a sort of stone wind tunnel in which grain was stacked. The farmer might also have experimented with crops newly introduced by the Romans: fruit and vegetables such as plums and crab-apples, peas, cabbages and carrots. Perhaps he also grew a patch of a new pot herb brought over by the Romans: ground elder.

Unfortunately it escaped and is still at large in our gardens.

One of the most interesting discoveries made in the area was that of two small hypocausts to the

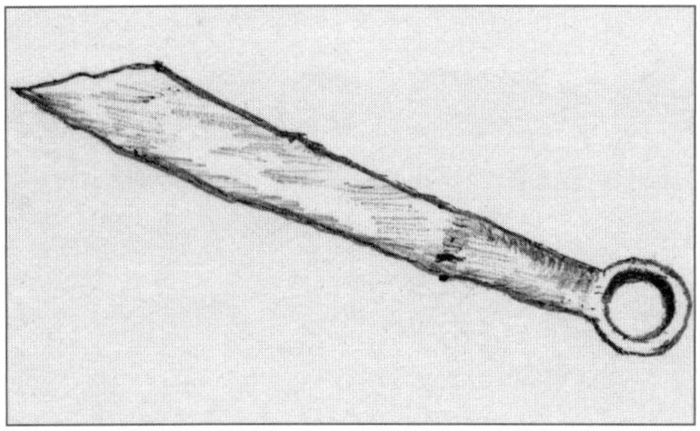

Iron knife (Roman), from Teffont Evias quarry.
Found by Ron Lever

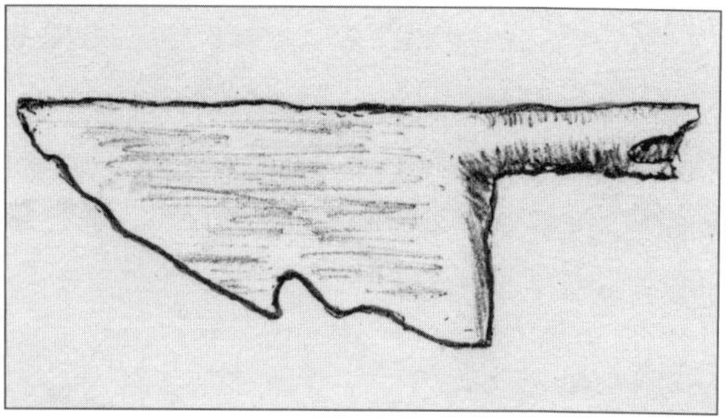

Butcher's chopper (Roman).
Found by Ron Lever

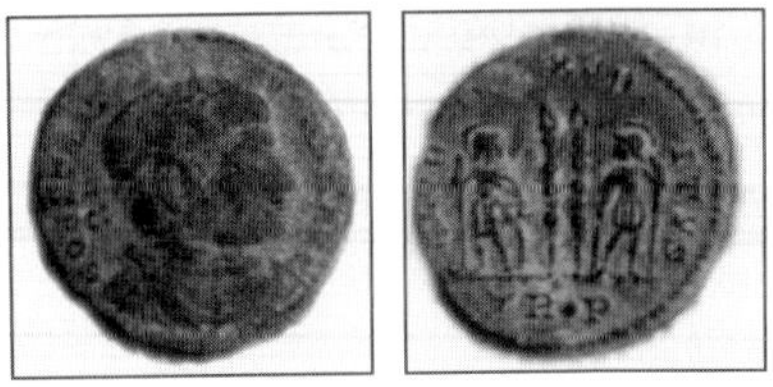

Roman coin. (EF)

west of the quarry area by R S Newall in 1935. He left detailed drawings of them. Although these have been studied by several experts, the function of the hypocausts has not been established. Too small for heating a dwelling or firing a lime kiln, they were perhaps associated with grain-dryers.

The most important Roman site in the parish is situated at Upper Holt. It is registered as an Ancient Monument and described as 'a Romano-British building/shrine'. It was first mentioned in 1913, when earthworks were identified there and 'much Roman pottery' was found. Cuttings were made into the large mound on the site in the 1920s, but no finds were made. Further digging to the west of the mound in 1959 revealed a chalk floor and other signs of building. More than 200 Roman coins and a large quantity of late Iron Age and Romano-British pottery shards were recovered.

The cache of coins supports the theory that it was a shrine (the coins having been left by devotees). On the other hand, the commanding view of the site, affording a 360 degree view over the surrounding countryside, has led to the proposal that it was a look-out post—a suggestion supported by the large amount of potsherds, often regarded as a clue to the presence of the Roman army, who were prodigious users of pottery. The site is now completely overgrown, but six copper coins were found by illegal use of a metal detector in 1985. It is interesting that each coin was minted under a different emperor; their dates range from 268 to 354 AD.

Pressure on the Roman Empire began to be felt in Britain towards the middle of the 4th century AD, and its authority began to crumble. The situation was temporarily restored by Theodosius in 367, but the Roman hold on the island gradually slackened in the course of the 5th century, leaving many areas bereft of administration or defence and vulnerable to attack by 'barbarians' (including those employed by the Roman army). Trade came to a standstill, the usage of coins was abandoned, and even the indigenous potteries ceased production. The farms in our district do not appear to have long survived this period.

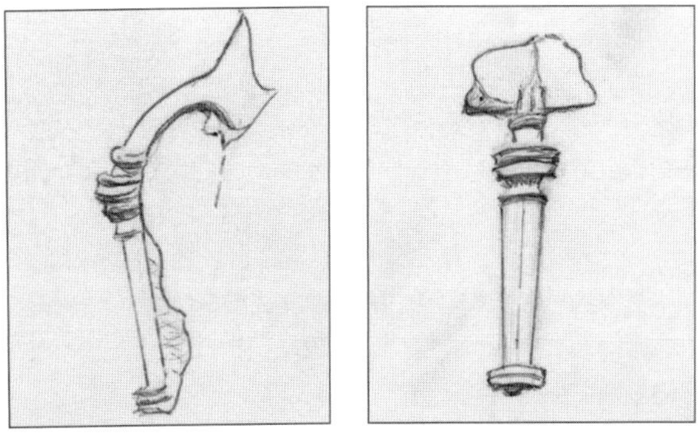

Romano-British trumpet brooch, found in Teffont Evias quarry.

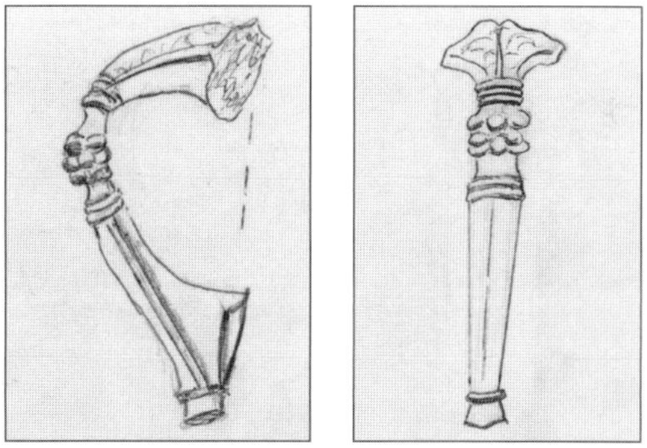

Romano-British trumpet brooch, found in Teffont Evias quarry.

CHAPTER THREE

A GLIMPSE INTO THE DARK AGES

To what extent the Germanic invasions, which began in the 5th century, were responsible for the demise of the Grovely Ridge farming settlements is not known. Probably they exacerbated the climate of depression and insecurity that the withdrawal of the Romans had brought. The local populace may also have found itself in an area of conflict. British resistance to the Germanic invaders was strongest in the west of the country under leaders such as Ambrosius Aurelianus and subsequently Arthur (if legend is to be believed.) Camelot has been identified as South Cadbury, and around 500 AD Arthur is said to have won a great battle at Badon Hill (thought to be in the region of Swindon). As the result of another battle not far away, however, Old Sarum fell to the invaders in 552, and fifty years later West Saxons were reported to have settled an area of the Wylye valley near Wilton. Since the Saxons apparently liked to make their settlements close to streams, using the lower slopes for ploughing and the upper for pasture, the British settlements may have been in their way.

Whatever the reason, the British, who had farmed the area, disappeared without trace into the obscurity of the Dark Ages. Neither is there any record of activity in our village between the 5th and 9th centuries. This does not necessarily mean that there was no early Anglo-Saxon presence. Indeed, the fact that the Roman suffix 'font' was coupled with 'tef', an old Frisian word for 'border', to give the village the name 'Teffont' argues for contact between the Romano-British and the Saxons. Also, it has been established that the later Saxons often built their villages on the sites of earlier hamlets. It may be, therefore, that the remains of such a hamlet lie beneath our village. A survey of Teffont by the Royal Commission for Historical Monuments in 1994 revealed a substantial quantity of Saxon earthworks below ground.

The early Saxon immigrants to Britain reverted, to a great extent, to the use of bio-degradable materials. They scorned the Roman stone villas, and built houses of timber and thatch. They also favoured implements, including tableware, made from wood. As a consequence, few traces of their habitations remain. Even where the sites of hamlets have been discovered, few artefacts have come to light. Pottery was usually of such poor quality and so low-fired that little of it survived. A few potsherds have,

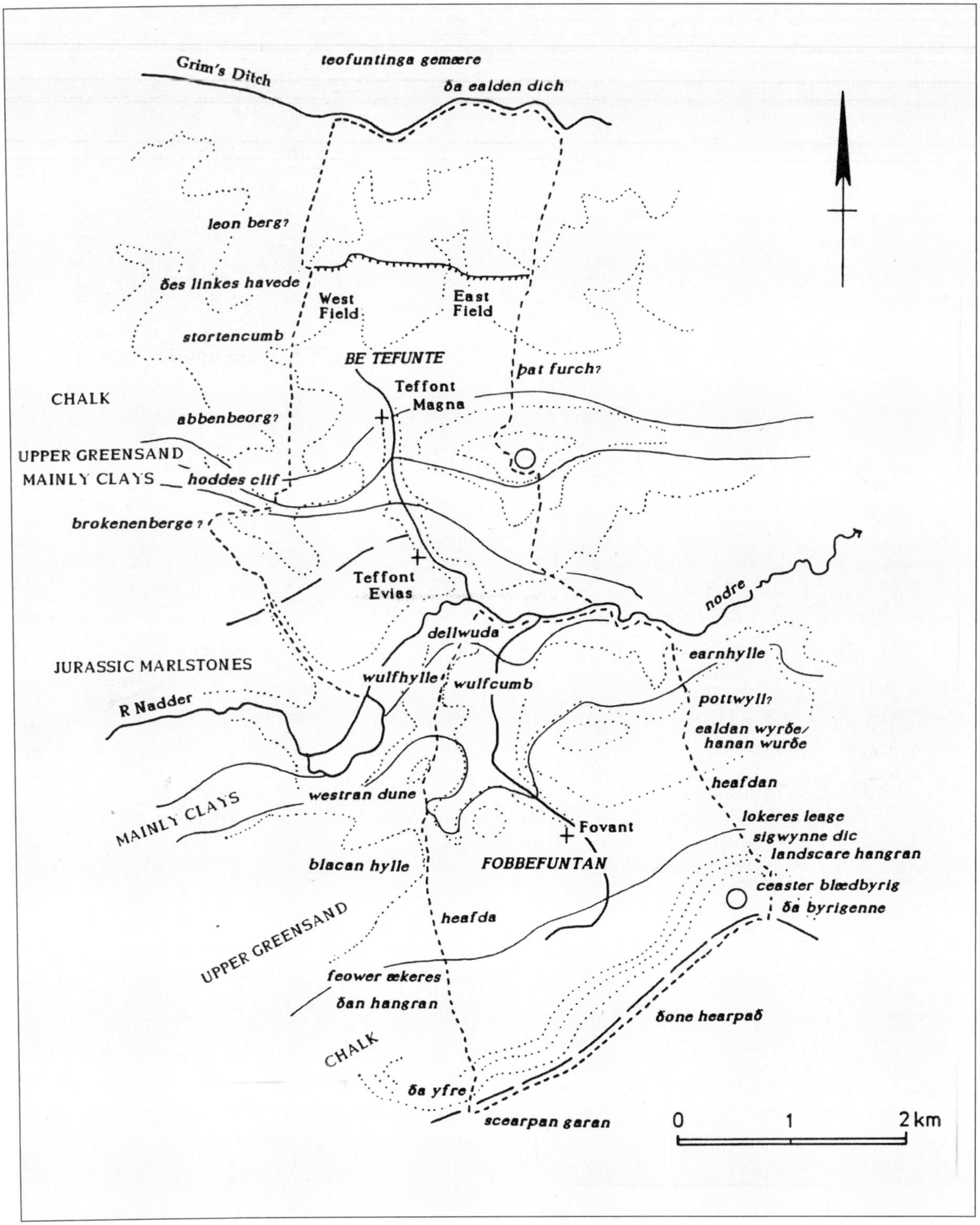

Reproduced by courtesy of Dr Della Hooke

however, been found in Teffont. Although some metal and horn implements were used, they were perhaps considered too valuable to leave around for later archaeologists to discover.

Burial grounds have provided a much richer source of artefacts, for the pagan Saxons liked to leave grave-goods for the comfort of the departed. These varied from a crude pot for the humble peasant to finely made weaponry for the nobleman—and perhaps a purpose-killed wife. Since coffins were not used and graves were unmarked, they are not easily discovered. None has been found in our area.

However, some notable graves have been discovered not far away on Swallowcliffe Down, the richest ever found in Wiltshire. Here, towards the end of the 7th century the remains of an obviously very wealthy woman had been interred in a Neolithic barrow. Even though the grave had been pillaged, it still yielded valuable artefacts, including jewellery and silver. The significance of the grave is that although the lady is isolated in death, she cannot have been in life. There must have been a considerable community in the area to support such a wealthy life-style.

The first written reference to Teffont to come to light is in a charter dated 860 AD granting 14 hides of land at 'Be Tefunte' in hereditary tenure by Aethelwolf, King of the West Saxons, to 'Osmond the thegn'. The boundaries of the land are sufficiently defined to indicate that it covered much of the area now occupied by Teffont Magna and Teffont Evias, and there are suggestions that some of this land was already under cultivation. Osmond, then, was our first lord of the manor. He was a 'superior minister' of King Aethelwolf, perhaps related to the King's first wife, Osborh. A condition of his charter was that he was responsible for making bridges, furnishing forts and supporting the King on 'military expeditions' when required.

Lower fragment of 9th-century stone cross. (PL)

One such military expedition would no doubt have been to meet the Viking invaders at Wilton in 871 AD. The Anglo-Saxon forces, under the command of King Alfred, unfortunately lost the battle. As a result our valley would most likely have suffered periodic pillaging by the Vikings until they were driven out of Wessex after Alfred's great victory at Edington in the year 878.

Apart from the potsherds mentioned above, the only artefacts of Saxon origin to have been found in the village are two mutilated blocks of carved limestone, one 57cm and the other 25cm in length. The first was found buried in a garden adjacent to the church in 1967; the second was found eight years later, built into a buttress of the church. They have been identified as 9th-century, probably King Alfred period. Although the interlace design differs slightly on each, they are believed to be fragments of the same cross-shaft. They have been set into the south wall of Teffont Magna church.

The stones obviously demonstrate a Christian tradition, although

Upper fragment of 9th-century stone cross showing figure-of-eight knot. (PL)

when Christianity came to the village and from what source is a matter for conjecture. Barry Cunliffe, the historian, suggests that Christianity was brought to Wessex around 635 AD by an Italian missionary named Birinus. Among the articles recovered from the 7th-century Swallowcliffe burial was a satchel decorated with a double-armed cross, demonstrating that Christian symbols were known in this area, even though the community was still pagan.

It is also possible that the faith was introduced from Ireland, where the carving of stone crosses was a feature of early Christianity. The intricate knot design on the cross-shaft is of Celtic origin. Known as 'runic', it developed from a growing vine, representing Christ's words: 'I am the true vine'. The figure-of-eight knots on the smaller fragment are not customary, however, and may be an exotic development.

Many such crosses have been found in towns and villages in England, and are thought to have originated as preaching crosses, where the first services were held. An alternative theory that they were grave-markers cannot be ignored, but appears less likely. Whatever the explanation, it is beyond doubt that the crosses stood on consecrated ground.

A second written reference to Teffont is contained in a grant made by King Edgar in the year 964 of five hides of land to a certain Sigestan. He was obviously a farming man, for his land appeared to be in scattered strips on common land. This is one of the earliest mentions of strip farming—the system whereby peasant farmers cultivated dispersed strips within the fields, while sharing grazing on common land. No location is given, but it is assumed to be a part of the 14 hides originally granted to Osmond.

So what happened to Osmond, the thegn, and his heirs? Although the grant gave him hereditary tenure, what the Crown gave, the Crown could easily take away. The pattern was set by Alfred himself. 'Great' though he was reputed to be, he was a ruthless monarch who imposed heavy tax burdens on his subjects; non-payment could result in the confiscation of their land.

Between this time and the Norman Conquest, significant changes took place in the ownership of our village. It is known that the northern part, now known as Teffont Magna, together with the manor of Dinton was given to Shaftesbury Abbey, which King Alfred had founded for his daughter, Aethelgifu. No written records of the transaction survive, but a mention in local history is made of 'five cassates (of land) at Teofunt' being given to the abbey in 966.

The end of the 10th century introduced a time of renewed conflict. The Vikings were on the warpath again, and Wessex was the scene of intermittent warfare. How close hostilities came to this area is not known, but it is significant that Wilton was burnt down in the year 1003. The wars were expensive in both men and material. Since the Danes were more often bought off than defeated, fewer men died, but religious houses and private estates alike were bled white to raise tribute money.

Hostilities were finally ended in 1016, when Cnut was crowned king. He was responsible for a major redistribution of property and power, replacing many of the old English thegns with others of his choosing. Among the latter was certainly Godwin, father of the future King Harold, and possibly Karlo, who became the first landlord of the southern part of Teffont; by this time it was separated, and would later become known as Teffont Evias.

The Danish victory brought to an end not only the rule of the Anglo-Saxon kings, but also the predominance of Wessex. However, the name of one of its noblest monarchs lives on in our village. When the church at Teffont Magna was dedicated in 1965, it was given the name of St Edward, king of the West Saxons—the young king who was murdered at Corfe Castle by his stepmother in 978. He was buried in Shaftesbury Abbey, and canonized in 1001. His tomb acquired a reputation for performing miracles, and consequently brought fame and fortune to the abbey.

Shaftesbury Abbey

CHAPTER FOUR

GOOD DAYS, BAD DAYS AND DOMESDAY

Unless there was active opposition to the invaders it is unlikely that our village was greatly affected by the Norman Conquest in 1066. Unlike the Vikings and the Saxons, the Normans did not come looking for land to farm. William the Conqueror sought the throne of England because he thought it was his right to rule what was obviously a prosperous and flourishing island.

English remained the language of the common people. William stressed the importance of continuity and the preservation of established customs. One in particular appealed to him: the system of general taxation. However, he decided that the time was ripe for a reassessment of the country's assets, and set in motion the Domesday inquest. In the course of it, the size and ownership of every estate and the amount of its assets were set out in detail. Those in the Salisbury area were recorded by the canons of the cathedral at Old Sarum.

All land now belonged to the crown. Most of the Saxon thegns had their land confiscated, and Norman nobles were appointed to take them over as tenants-in-chief of the crown. They in turn rented out their land to lesser lords, and small plots of it came down to the peasantry. Under the system every man had to have a master. The structure was already in place during the Saxon era, but the Normans proved to be harder and more rapacious masters than their Saxon predecessors.

A few bishops and abbots, including Leogifu, Abbess of Shaftesbury, were allowed to retain their estates. As can be seen from the Domesday survey, the abbey lands were widespread. Teffont Magna is not mentioned in the record, but it is understood to have been included in the 20 hides attributed to Dinton. Of these, 7 hides were in the Abbey's demesne, 2 were held by Gunfrid Maldit (a minor Norman baron), and the remaining 11 were farmed by tenants. These tenants comprised 21 villeins and 10 bordars, employing 11 ploughs. There were 20 acres of meadow, the same area of woodland, 1.5 leagues of pasture and 2 mills.

Teffont Evias is not mentioned under its full name in Domesday. It is referred to simply as 'Tefunte'. However, it is recorded as one of the manors of the powerful Baron Alfred (or Alured) of Marlborough, whose main seat was Ewyas Castle in Hereford. (The name 'Ewyas' is a local one, meaning 'sheep valley'). The origin of the village's name is plain; Ewyas is the first recorded spelling of Evias.

Ewyas Castle was one of the first castles in England. A timber construction based on a French design, it had been built in the early 11th century by Osbern Pentecost, one of a colony of Norman nobles, favourites of King Edward I, who were established in Hereford, on the Welsh border. The Normans needed to fortify themselves, since they were hated by the English on one side and the Welsh on the other. They were especially hated by Godwin, Earl of Wessex, who eventually defeated them in battle. Osbern escaped and fled to Scotland, where in 1054 he died fighting with Shakespeare's anti-hero, King Macbeth.

The tables were turned after the Norman Conquest. Then Alfred of Marlborough, who was Osbern's nephew, had Ewyas Castle restored to him, together with enough additional estates to make him one of the richest of King William's tenants-in-chief. These included many of Karlo's estates, including Teffont. What became of Karlo is not known. No doubt he suffered one of the three options available to the Anglo-Saxon land-owner: either he was killed, or he fled the country, or he became a humble tenant on one of his own estates.

Alfred had no connections with the Wiltshire town of Marlborough. He may have taken the name from a hamlet of that name on his Welsh estate.

Site of Ewyas Harold Castle, built by Osbern Pentecost (11th century).

Teffont Ewyas was one of a number of smaller manors formerly held by Karlo, inherited by the Baron. Although King William was generous in bestowing land on his favourites, he made sure that they were dispersed throughout the country rather than contiguous, so that they could not be developed into large estates capable of threatening his authority. In the Domesday Book the area of 'Tefunte' is given as 6.5 hides, 2.5 of which were tenanted by 4 villeins, 3 bordars and 1 immigrant Frenchman, using 2 plough teams. It had 6 acres each of meadow, pasture and woodland, and one mill.

By fleshing out the bare bones provided by Domesday, a glimpse of life in our parish in the 11th century can be obtained. The northern area (Teffont Magna), linked to Dinton, comprised 11 hides leased to peasant farmers, 31 in all; these were men with families living in thatched mud-and-wattle houses, farming enough land to warrant the use of 11 ploughs (each with a team of 8 oxen). The 21 villeins would have had strip fields in which were grown wheat, barley, oats and beans on a crop rotation basis, fertilized by grazing sheep. The bordars were restricted to

Tomb of Robert Ewias, Abbeydore.

small-holdings producing vegetables, with perhaps some fruit and chickens. The pasture was common land for grazing cows, oxen, sheep and horses. The meadow (by the river) was used for further grazing and also for hay-making, while the woodland provided timber, fuel and pasturing for swine.

In the 11th century, water-driven grinding mills had replaced the old rotary querns. They were a big leap forward, but had certain disadvantages. The villeins were required to pay for the service of the manorial mill—Dalwood in the case of Teffont. The millers were notorious for exacting unfair payments and corrupting the flour.

This payment was one of a number of contributions exacted from the villeins as rent for their land. These varied from manor to manor. Among the services which might be expected of them were 1 to 3 days labour per week, annual cash payments, tributes of garden produce and payment for pannage in the forest. Nevertheless, some of the villeins were reasonably well-off and enjoyed a certain status: they were eligible to serve as jurors, and certain officials, such as the reeve (the working bailiff) were drawn from their ranks.

The pattern of life at the Ewyas end of the parish would not have been dissimilar, although the community was much smaller: just 7 peasant families. The Frenchman mentioned in Domesday was very likely the Norman bailiff in charge of Marlborough's estate. The Baron would have paid regular visits, staying for several days and eating the food produced by the 9 serfs on his demesne, supplemented by produce from his tenants' fields. (The original meaning of the word 'farmer' was a villein who held land on condition that he supplied food to his lord when visiting).

However, Marlborough was not allowed to enjoy his visits for very long. Either as a result of death or disgrace, he disappeared only two years after the Domesday inquest. The greater part of his estate (including Teffont) was granted to Harold, Lord of Sudely, whose name became associated with the Barony of Ewyas.

The fact that the two sides of the village were in the possession of different landlords and in different hundreds did not necessarily mean that their inhabitants were isolated from one another. There were no physical boundaries, and it probably made little difference to the tenants whether they paid a portion of the fruits of their hard labour to the baron or the abbess. It is unlikely that they met as strangers.

They would certainly have experienced the same hardships. These were especially severe during the last years of the 11th century, which appear to have been a heavy rain phase. The statement 'heavy rains which did not cease all year' in the Anglo-Saxon Chronicle for 1098 is typical. The result was a succession of poor harvests, resulting in hungry winters. The villagers of Teffont could not even supplement their meagre fare by hunting in the forest, since this was only permitted to Norman nobles, and the poaching of deer, or of the newly introduced rabbits, incurred a heavy penalty. A poacher caught red-handed could almost certainly expect to end up on the gibbet.

Although there is no record of a church in the locality, it is inconceivable that there was not one. By the 11th century every community had access to a church, not only for the administration of the sacraments, but also as a meeting-place. Since it was not recorded in Domesday, it is likely to have been a 'stocken' church—a simple wooden building with thatched roof. The priest was probably included among the villeins (this was common practice). The area of Teffont Magna suggests itself as a likely site, since the Saxon stone cross found there is evidence of consecrated ground. Cut stones of the 11th or 12th century unearthed near the church (and now on display inside it) are evidence of an earlier building, whose foundations were revealed when main drainage was laid on in Teffont Magna in 1977. It is significant that a layer of what appeared to be burnt material was observed below the foundations, suggesting that they had replaced a wooden construction which had been burnt down. The capacious barrel-shaped (though cut-down) stone font in the church dates back to Norman times, or perhaps earlier.

It is possible that a church had already been established in Teffont Ewyas, for the lords of Ewyas had a reputation for piety. In 1100 Harold of Ewyas granted the tithes of certain of his manors including

Teffont Magna church, 13th-century. (Porch added 14th century).

Interior of Teffont Magna church. (PL)

'Tedfunde' to St Peter's Abbey, Gloucester, which at the time of the Conquest was almost completely run down. The King himself (Henry I) led a campaign to rebuild it, and Harold of Ewyas was among the landowners who followed his lead. Our village may therefore claim the credit for having contributed, to a small degree, to the restoration of the ancient abbey.

In 1136 Henry I died, and civil war broke out. Although, so far as we know, Teffont was not involved in the dispute between the rival heirs to the throne (Stephen and his cousin Matilda), the community cannot fail to have suffered as a result of being between the two warring factions. Not only were there violent battles in Wiltshire, but there was also looting and pillaging throughout the land by undisciplined soldiers. A quarter of the county was laid to waste, and Wilton was once again burnt to the ground.

In Hereford, Robert, the overlord of Teffont Ewyas (he had succeeded his father, Harold, to the Barony) was a supporter of King Stephen. He led an army on the King's behalf to quash a Welsh rebellion. His army may have included Teffont villagers, for men were recruited from the Wiltshire villages. Perhaps it was as a consequence of this costly exercise that Robert of Ewyas parcelled out a number of his estates as knights' 'fees'.

One of these estates was Teffont, which between 1150 and 1166 was granted to a nephew, Godfrey. He subsequently assumed the title 'Godfrey de Tifente'. Thus Teffont Ewyas finally became a recognized manor with its own resident lord.

Even though stability was restored after the accession of the first Plantagenet king, Henry II, in 1154, the country remained in a state of economic depression for many years. Agricultural prices sank to such an extent that many landowners gave up cultivating their demesnes and demanded rent in money rather than labour from their tenants. The Abbess of Shaftesbury was not among these; continued cultivation was necessary in order to provide the increasing number of nuns and their dependants with food and drink. Dalwood Mill had become a malt mill, and one of the Teffont villeins' tasks was to transport malted grain to the abbey for the production of the nuns' ale.

Whether or not Godfrey de Ewyas continued to cultivate his demesne is not known, but it seems likely that he built a manor house in Teffont Ewyas, and (if there was not one there already) at least began building a church for his family and tenants. The extensive 19th-century restoration of Teffont Evias church made it impossible to establish when it was originally constructed. The font, however, is dated c1200, and repairs to the church after flooding in 1999 revealed a 13th-century piscina. Its location in the south wall at the front of the nave suggests that the altar was originally sited nearby. This strengthens the likelihood of the church having developed from an earlier building, since according to David Hinton, the altar in early medieval churches customarily stood at the front of the nave.

The stone foundations uncovered in 1977 beside the 13th-century church at Teffont Magna (mentioned above) indicate the existence of a larger earlier church. As it stands today, the church is a single-cell rectangular building, which has sometimes been likened to a barn (not a description we encourage!). Most early medieval churches were double-cell buildings, consisting of a rectangular nave with a smaller square or semi-circular chancel at the east end. Since buried foundations were uncovered outside the east end of the church, it seems possible that they are the remains of a second cell. By 1225 the church had become a chapel subordinate to Dinton, and no longer had its own priest, and hence there would no longer have been a requirement for a chancel. Since the upkeep of the chancel was the responsibility of the priest, while the parishioners maintained the nave, it is quite possible that it fell into disrepair and was pulled down. It is perhaps significant that while the main structure of the church is built of rubble, the east wall is constructed of larger stones.

Teffont Magna church font. (PL)

The Dinton church appears to have been held in high regard. An occasion is recorded when its rector was nominated by the Bishop of Salisbury to 'enjoin salutary penance to delinquent nuns' in Shaftesbury Abbey. The nature of their delinquency is not divulged. However, nuns of this period were not renowned for their piety, most of them having taken the veil for reasons of expediency rather than a sense of vocation. The task of disciplining them may not have been an easy one, since they probably considered themselves to be socially a cut above the rector of one of the abbey's less important estates.

Whatever effect he had on the nuns of Shaftesbury, the rector of Dinton would doubtless have inspired awe in the breasts of his parishioners in Dinton and Teffont. Unlike the early Christian missionaries, the medieval clergy preached not the love but the fear of God—a message reinforced by paintings of the torments of hell which decorated the walls of the local churches.

Teffont Evias church font. (VK)

There appears to have been little local awareness of the political power struggle which was currently taking place between King John and his barons. It would, of course, have been of little concern to the villains, but surely of some interest to the occupants of Teffont Ewyas manor, the descendants of the Ewyas barony. It is quite possible that Robert de Tregoze, who had inherited the barony, intended to be among the barons who witnessed the sealing of Magna Carta in 1215, for he was a close associate of the Earl of Pembroke; but he had died a few months earlier.

The death of Godfrey de Ewyas resulted in a split in the ownership of the manor.

It was jointly inherited by his granddaughters, Philippe and Parnel, whose shares descended through different families until the end of the century. Their overlord in Ewyas Harold, the second Baron Robert de Tregoze, died at Evesham in 1265 while supporting Simon de Montfort in the last of the Barons' Wars against Henry III. His son, John de Tregoze, having succeeded in gaining his monarch's forgiveness for his father's treason, staunchly supported the king in many battles, and provided him with horses. He died in 1300.

The early years of the 13th century had brought a turn-around in the agricultural market. There were good harvests, an increasing population stimulated demand, and agricultural prices rose rapidly. Landlords, both secular and ecclesiastical, were quick to jump on the band-wagon, re-cultivating their demesnes and demanding labour once again rather than money as rent from their tenants. A market economy was established, chiefly based on wheat; and as the century progressed, demesne farming became ever more intensive. More woodland was cleared, and every available piece of land was pressed into service.

The labour demanded of the villeins of Teffont Magna steadily increased, to include in addition to the customary ploughing and harvesting, manure-spreading, regular weeding of the corn fields, and transporting produce to market or for storage in the great barn which the abbey had erected at Tisbury (it still stands today).

However, the villeins shared to some degree in the growing prosperity. The Lay Subsidy Rolls of 1225 listed the 'moveable assets' of all tenant farmers for taxation purposes. We are fortunate that the Rolls covering the manors of Dinton and Teffont (Magna) are among the few which still survive. Although

'Teffunt' is described as belonging to the manor of Dinton, its 37 tenants are listed separately from the 41 of Dinton. Each is named with the amount and value of taxable stock that he owned.

Between them, the 37 villeins owned upwards of 60 cows and heifers and more than 400 sheep, in addition to bullocks, pigs and horses. They also had sizeable quantities of oats and barley. Two of the villeins had hives (until the 13th century a prerogative of the demesne), thereby giving the community ready access to a supply of honey, the only known sweetener. The tenant with the highest tax bill was Adam Awelma, with 2 shillings to pay on 1 horse, 2 cows, 3 bullocks, 1 heifer, 33 sheep and a quantity of barley, altogether valued at 30 shillings.

Unfortunately, the Lay Subsidy Rolls covering Teffont Ewyas have not survived, but it might be supposed that the community there was also enjoying the agricultural boom. Some of the villeins may have supplemented their income by working in the quarries. Between 1200 and 1259 the new cathedral in Salisbury was being built, and 60,000 tons of Chilmark/Tisbury stone was used in its construction. Working in the quarries was a hazardous business, but injured workers at least had the advantage of access to the unprecedented medical attention offered by the Knights Hospitallers, who had set up a hospital at nearby Ansty.

13th-century church bell in Teffont Magna church, one of the oldest in England. (PL)

It was fortuitous that the Wiltshire farmers were able to get a foot in the door of the burgeoning wool trade. Hitherto sheep had been primarily regarded as walking bags of fertilizer, and the flocks had been built up to enable a wider use of the poor chalkland soil for grain production. The opportunity to turn the surplus wool into profit was a welcome bonus. The marketing of the wool had become highly organized, and Teffont Ewyas was involved in a scheme of exchange between various manors specializing in different stages of sheep rearing to ensure the quality of the flocks.

It could be said of the villeins of the Teffonts that 'they had never had it so good' as during the second half of the 13th century. But in this context, 'good' meant no more for many of them than managing to stay above the breadline.

CHAPTER FIVE

FROM BLACK DEATH TO CLOTH OF GOLD

The good times did not continue beyond the end of the 13th century. The seeds of disaster had already been sown during the bumper harvests. The profitable market for wheat had led to too much land being forced into cultivation. By the end of the century much of the marginal soil was becoming exhausted, and a new phase of cold, wet weather set in. There was a slow deterioration until 1315, when heavy rain caused the first of a succession of failed harvests. The landlords cut their losses by once again abandoning the cultivation of their demesnes and demanding rent in place of labour from their villein tenants. But this time it was an expedient which would eventually rebound on them, and lead to the demise of the feudal system.

Meanwhile the demand for rent constituted one more burden on the shoulders of the wretched villeins. Their situation had become desperate. Not only had the incessant rain ruined their crops and flooded their dwellings, but murrain had spread through the animal herds. This is usually interpreted as foot-and-mouth disease, but it could also be the potentially fatal rinderpest or cow-pox. Then a further curse was visited upon them: bubonic plague—the Black Death.

It was brought into Wessex on the backs of rats from a ship docked at Melcombe Regis in the summer of 1348, and it spread through the ill-nourished population like flames through a stubble field. They attributed it to the wrath of God, provoked by their own sinfulness, never suspecting the vermin which infested their insanitary dwellings.

There is no record of the death toll in the Teffonts. Historians often base such estimates on the rate of replacement of clergy in the episcopal rolls of the period; in some parishes this was as many as four in the course of twelve months. It came as a profound shock to the common people that God should scourge his chosen vicars with such ferocity, and brought about the first cracks in their unquestioning faith in the infallibility of the clergy. Although it was not until the 16th century that the Protestant movement got off the ground, the first seeds of Protestantism were undoubtedly sown at the time of the Black Death.

The indications are that this area might have suffered less than the average. The appointment of two vicars in Teffont Ewyas in 1349—John Chaunders followed by Walter Miles—may have had sinister implications, but in Dinton, Johannes de Kynmerick remained in his pulpit from 1342 to 1354.

As a result of bad management, combined with housing too many nuns, Shaftesbury Abbey had been losing money even during the boom years. By the middle of the century it was badly in debt. Joan Fromage, the abbess, appeared to blame this to some extent on the Black Death. In a begging letter to the King, she cited 'the pestilence which has caused great mortality among our tenants and the murrain of their cattle' as reasons for their financial embarrassment. The nuns themselves appear to have escaped the plague, probably as a result of being a closed order and living within a well-built stone building which the rats could not easily penetrate.

Whether the plague afflicted the lords of Teffont Ewyas is not known. Although landlords lived in more salubrious surroundings than their tenants, the fact that their houses were mainly of timber made them vulnerable to infiltration by rats. But they had the advantage of being able to move away when the plague arrived.

Indeed, there would have been occasions when they were forced to leave. In 1337 the heads of the Hussey and Horton families—who, between them, owed a knight's fee to their Hereford overlords for the lordship of Teffont Ewyas—would have been required to follow the King (Edward III) to Normandy for the first campaigns of the Hundred Years War against the French. A few years earlier, Reginald Husie had incurred the wrath of William de Grandison (who had succeeded to the Hereford overlordship) as a result of failing to fulfil his obligation to undertake guard-duty at Ewyas Harold Castle, and was punished by being fined of a number of cattle.

Despite a recurrence of the plague in 1361, the agricultural communities began a steady resurgence. There was, however, a chronic shortage of labour on the demesne lands, a situation which put the villeins at an unusual advantage: since they no longer owed labour as rent to their landlords, they could sell their services to the highest bidder. The government introduced laws to control agricultural wages, which led to great outrage and culminated in the Peasants' Revolt in 1381. Most of the Wessex landlords, however, appear to have taken the line of least resistance. They leased their agrarian land at low rents to their tenants, and concentrated their efforts on the increasingly lucrative and less labour-intensive business of sheep farming. The steadily expanding market for wool provided a step-ladder by which entrepreneurial families could reach the ranks of the nobility.

One such was the Hungerford family. Although at his birth in 1325 Thomas Hungerford inherited neither money nor status, when he died in 1397 he was one of the wealthiest and most influential knights in Wiltshire. How he laid the foundations of his fortune is not clear. However, his appointment as chief steward of all the lands of John of Gaunt, Duke of Lancaster may have made a substantial contribution, enabling him to buy several manors, including Heytesbury, in rich, sheep-rearing country. He became the county sheriff of Wiltshire in 1365 and the first Speaker of the House of Commons in 1377.

Sir Thomas Hungerford is of especial interest to our village since in around 1377 he married Joan, heiress to the Hussey portion of Teffont Ewyas manor. It was a second marriage for both of them, but while Thomas was over fifty, Joan was still a young woman; the following year she gave birth to a son, who would grow up to be the illustrious Lord Hungerford. Even though by this time Sir Thomas owned another twenty or so estates, he bought out the Hortons, who still owned a part of Teffont Ewyas, and thus established complete ownership of the manor. Since for most of the time the demesne lands were leased out, it is doubtful if he ever took up residence here; it is more likely that he took Joan off to live in his newly-built castle at Hungerford Farleigh, returning no doubt from time to time to sample the fruits of his demesne and the tributes owed to him by his tenant farmers.

Most of the Hungerford land was dedicated to wool production. The breeding flocks were kept in Somerset, but were subsequently sent for grazing on the chalklands of the Wiltshire estates. They may have contributed to the notable success achieved by the Teffont Ewyas tenant farmers, who were among the first in the county to work a three-field system; they regularly marketed between a quarter and a third of their production. This may well have been due to the introduction into Teffont farming of the concept of 'sheep/corn agriculture', in which the corn fields were fertilized by folding large numbers of sheep on them overnight. It was to become the accepted method of farming in our area until the introduction of artificial fertilizers in the 20th century.

The latter part of the 14th century was the time when the wool industry moved out of the towns into the country. The Teffont villagers would already have been very familiar with the process of converting sheeps' wool into fabric. In early medieval pictures, a peasant's wife is often seen with a distaff in her hand. The yarn she produced was woven on a primitive loom, fulled by being trampled upon in water from the stream, dried and finally teased, using the teasels which grew on the banks. The resulting cloth was coarse and rough, but an effective barrier against the cold.

The products of the wool merchants were more refined. The main reason they moved to the country was the discovery of the suitability of the fast-flowing chalk streams for the working of fulling-mills. Many new mills were built, and established grist-mills were converted to fulling.

Scratching of a ship inside the porch of Teffont Magna church. (PL)

Thomas Hungerford bought

Dalwood Mill in Dinton for this purpose. Access to mills made fulling quicker and easier than trampling the cloth. The disadvantage for the villagers was that—as with the grist mill—they were required to use the manorial fulling mill and pay for the privilege. The villeins of Teffont Magna most likely used Shaftesbury Abbey's tucking mill in Tisbury. (The name, but not the mill, can still be seen there).

The village women were at least able to enjoy the unprecedented experience of making a little money by the use of their distaffs or spinning wheels. The merchants contracted out to the villages much of the carding and spinning of their (higher quality) wool. A great deal of it was exported to the continent as yarn.

The fact that a porch was added to Teffont Magna church in the 14th century indicates that there was a little money to spare. Scratchings of medieval vessels on its walls suggest that some sons of the village went to sea. They may perhaps have served as hands on the ships used in the thriving wool export trade from Southampton to continental ports.

The bulk of the profits went into the pockets of the merchants and landowners. The Hungerfords went from strength to strength. There can be few men who achieved their fathers' ambitions for them to the extent of Thomas's son, Walter. He achieved distinction both in the field of battle and the realm of scholarship.

Angel bearing a shield, in Teffont Evias church. (PL)

Like his father before him, he became sheriff of Wiltshire and Speaker of the House of Commons. He fought at Agincourt, where he captured the Duke of Orleans, whose ransom, it is said, enabled him to buy another thirty or so manors and to enlarge and embellish Farleigh Castle. He was a skilled Latinist and patronised Merton College in Oxford. A favourite of King Henry V, he served as both an admiral and an ambassador. He was appointed a Knight of the Garter, was raised to the peerage, and established the Hungerfords as the foremost of the county families of Wiltshire.

It is surprising that despite his numerous other commitments, Walter took a personal interest in his Teffont Ewyas demesne. Although the warren, with its valuable colony of rabbits (a delicacy introduced by the Normans) and a couple of fish-ponds were leased out (to the villeins, one hopes!), the farmland was incorporated into the Hungerford sheep-raising network.

In 1424, just before Walter was ennobled and appointed Lord Treasurer to King Henry VI, the Hungerford family paid a visit to Teffont Ewyas, and stayed long enough to make a serious dent in the grain stores.

Since Lord Hungerford had a reputation for piety and made many gifts to the church in general, it is strange that he has left no identifiable mark on the Teffont Ewyas church. However, there is evidence of building during the 15th century, notably the finely carved wooden roof over the area at the east end of the north aisle, known as the Ley Chapel. Before its incorporation into the north aisle in the 19th century, it was a side chapel, and was very likely built originally as a private or chantry chapel for the Hungerfords. The small, typically 15th-century figures of angels bearing shields which sit rather uncomfortably on the capitals of the columns in the main aisle might once have adorned such a chapel. It would not be surprising if all traces of the Hungerfords were removed during the 16th century, for it was then that chantries were abolished (as a consequence of the Reformation), and Henry Ley became lord of the manor of Teffont Ewyas.

The 15th-century Ley Chapel in Teffont Evias church. (VK)

Little is recorded of the life of Walter's son, Robert, beyond the fact that he married a wealthy heiress: Margaret, daughter of Lord Botreaux. He has sometimes been described as 'colourless'. The feet of his effigy in Salisbury Cathedral resting on a hound, with a special hunting leash, suggest that hunting was his main pleasure.

His son, also Robert (who acquired the title Lord Molyns and Hungerford), was a very different character. After a stormy adolescence he went off to France, where the last battles of the Hundred Years War were raging. He was captured by the French in Gascony in 1452. Perhaps recalling the ransom paid to Robert's grandfather for the release of the Duke of Orleans, the French put a high price-tag on him: £12,000. In order to raise the ransom, his mother had to sell the family silver and mortgage some of her estates. One small compensation was that on his release seven years later, Robert was allowed to export 1,500 sacks of wool from the Wiltshire estates without paying duty.

He did not stay at home for long. The Wars of the Roses had broken out in England. The Hungerfords were staunch Lancastrians, so he rode off to support King Henry VI. He survived several battles, but was captured after King Henry's defeat at Hexham in 1461. When the Yorkist Edward IV was proclaimed the rightful king, the Hungerfords were treated as traitors. Robert was executed, an attainder was placed on the Hungerford estates and most of the land—including the manor of Teffont Ewyas—was seized by Richard, the notorious Duke of Gloucester. Five years later the Hungerford heir, Thomas, was executed as a consequence of his involvement in an unsuccessful uprising against the Yorkist regime.

Effigy of Robert Hungerford in Salisbury Cathedral. (VK)

The sun might have set forever over the Hungerford empire had it not been for Thomas's grandmother, Margaret Botreaux. By this time she was an elderly widow who had lost both her son and grandson to the executioner, and one might have expected her to retire with her sorrows into a convent. But Margaret was made of sterner stuff. She was determined to regain the Hungerford title and property, and she fought tooth and nail to do so for the rest of her days. While she managed from time to time to wring a few concessions from Gloucester, including the temporary restoration of Teffont Ewyas manor, she was also frequently reviled and three times thrown into prison. Nevertheless, she persevered; although she did not live to see it, the attainder was reversed after her tormenter—now King Richard III—was slain and the crown given to Henry Tudor in 1485.

The barony descended to Thomas's daughter, Mary, married to Sir Edward Hastings, but most of the Hungerford estates were restored to Thomas's younger brother, Walter, who had been knighted on the battlefield at Bosworth. So it was as Sir Walter Hungerford that he became lord of the manor of Teffont Ewyas.

Although the Hungerford family, and many other noble families of Wiltshire, suffered grievously as a result of the Wars of the Roses, it appears that by and large, the common people were little affected. In fact the Teffont Ewyas tenants appear to have gained from the misfortunes of their landlords. The rents demanded for their land were reduced substantially between 1449 and 1474. The only indication we have of the dominion of the Duke of Gloucester is that in 1475 William Studard, the current incumbent, lost his job, and the living of the church was given to the Prior of Lechlade. In view of the distance involved, one can only suppose that he appointed a curate to take the services—a man, perhaps, with proven Yorkist sympathies.

Shaftesbury Abbey's financial situation recovered steadily in the 15th century, chiefly as a result of a reduction in the number of nuns from more than a hundred to fewer than fifty. It is surprising that unlike many other monasteries, it does not appear to have acquired a significant stake in the wool market.

The 15th century was the golden age for the wool trade in Wessex, and it brought riches to many of its clothiers. The principal export was now woollen cloth, rather than raw wool, and Salisbury became a major supplier. Although it seems unlikely that much of the riches filtered down to the humble spinners and weavers employed by the merchants, it is on record that the Salisbury market dealt not only in the fine quality cloths but also with the rougher weaves produced by the cottage industries in the surrounding villages. Evidence of local production of finished fabric in our area is furnished by the existence of the fulling mills, and also by the fact that there were two weavers in business in Tisbury, one employing 4 assistants. So it may be that although our villagers would not have known a golden age, they may at least have earned a few coppers during those times.

Hurdles of similar type to those used to fold sheep from the 14th to the 20th centuries.

CHAPTER SIX

TIP-TOEING THROUGH THE TUDORS

The dawn of the 16th century must have looked encouragingly bright in the Nadder Valley. The civil war was over; harvests were good; the wool trade was still booming; the Hungerfords were restored to favour, with their appointed incumbent in the pulpit of Ewyas church; and Shaftesbury Abbey was deemed to be the wealthiest nunnery in the kingdom. The storm clouds which were to wreak such havoc in the land were not yet visible above the horizon.

The disasters which were to strike the Hungerford family and Shaftesbury Abbey towards the middle of the century were, in a curious way, interlinked.

Although Sir Walter Hungerford did not die until 1516, he settled some of his estates, including Teffont Ewyas, on his son Edward in 1487. Sir Edward was apparently an upright and respected man; he was knighted at Tournai and was subsequently appointed Sheriff of Wiltshire, Somerset and Dorset. He obviously took a direct interest in his Teffont property, since he re-roofed part of the manor house, using tiles cut from Goldens quarry (one of the working quarries on his estate).

Soon after Sir Edward's death in 1523, however, a skeleton fell out of the Hungerford cupboard. Agnes, his second wife, was charged with the murder of her first husband in 1518, found guilty and hanged. Although Sir Edward was not implicated, the fact that the murder had taken place in his castle at Farleigh, that Agnes had been aided by yeomen of Heytesbury, and that Edward married her as soon as the corpse had been disposed of, suggests that he might not have been wholly dissociated. Despite this implication, the court took no proceedings against him, so perhaps we should give him the benefit of the doubt.

It would be difficult to treat his son (by his first wife, Jane Zouche) with as much magnanimity. At the time of his father's death, Walter Hungerford was nineteen years old and a squire at the court of Henry VIII. In the course of the next nine years he married and lost two wives. Then, in 1532, he married a descendant of the Hussey family—Elizabeth. Through her father he obtained an introduction to the notorious Thomas Cromwell, and as a result he was appointed Sheriff of Wiltshire. In this capacity he is reported to have 'proved useful' to Cromwell. In what way is not recorded, but the fact that Cromwell's chief occupation at the time was the dissolution of the monasteries may not be without significance. As a reward for his usefulness, Hungerford was given a barony. He continued to prosper under Cromwell's patronage until in 1540 Cromwell incurred the King's displeasure and was executed. Lord Hungerford lost his head on the block at the same time.

An insight into Walter Hungerford's character is demonstrated by his treatment of his wife. Elizabeth wrote desperate letters describing how she was incarcerated for years at a stretch in Farleigh Castle, and how several attempts were made to poison her.

Meanwhile the nuns of Shaftesbury Abbey were frantically trying to avoid being driven out. Already in 1529 they had glimpsed the writing on the wall when Henry VIII set up a commission under Cromwell to inspect the religious houses; Cromwell had demanded of them a gift of '2 beeves and 20 muttons' and the relinquishing of certain rights. The newly appointed abbess was Elizabeth Zouche, a relative of Walter Hungerford's own mother—perhaps his cousin, or even his aunt. But the abbess clearly gained no favours from the relationship. The orders for the complete dissolution of the abbey were served on her in 1539. She was persuaded to sign a deed of submission, handing over the abbey -lock, stock and barrel- to the King in exchange for a tiny pension for herself and her nuns.

Thus the two Teffonts lost their landlords within a year of each other; Thomas Cromwell was in one way or another responsible for the downfall of both of them. The bulk of the Hungerford estates was restored to a subsequent generation of the family by Queen Mary I, but this restoration did not include Teffont Ewyas, and an attempt by the Hungerfords to reclaim it in 1560 was unsuccessful.

The Shaftesbury Abbey lands passed first into the possession of the Duke of Somerset. A brother of Henry VIII's third queen, Jane Seymour, he was appointed Regent when his nine-year old nephew Edward VI ascended the throne in 1547, but he subsequently fell from grace and was executed in 1552.

It was as a result of his death that Teffont Magna began its long association with the Pembroke dynasty.

The founder of the dynasty was William Herbert (who, by an odd coincidence, was born in Ewyas Harold). His career had got off to an inauspicious start: he was involved in a fight in which a man was killed, so he was forced to hide away in France until the trouble blew over. The marriage he made on his return to England did not look very promising either: his bride, Ann Parr, had neither a large fortune nor great expectations. But then the unexpected happened: Henry VIII took her sister, Katherine, as his sixth queen. Then the good times began. The king showered his new brother-in-law with gifts, including a knighthood and the extensive estates of the newly dissolved Wilton Abbey.

During the short reign of Edward VI, William Herbert received further favours and gained both wealth and power, sometimes showing a certain contempt for moral scruples. He was created Earl of Pembroke in 1552, and shortly afterwards bought the Shaftesbury Abbey estates (including Dinton/Teffont Magna) for £8,440 7s 31/2d.

Herbert came close to disaster after King Edward's death as a consequence of supporting Lady Jane's claim to the throne; he was indeed one of the five peers who did homage to her during her eleven days as queen. However, he saw the writing on the wall in time to make a smart U-turn and declare his allegiance to Mary Tudor before Jane was brought to the scaffold. Later, during the reign of Queen Elizabeth, he had another narrow escape as a result of being involved in a scheme to arrange a marriage between Mary, Queen of Scots, and the Duke of Norfolk. However, by means of some nimble footwork he was able to emerge unscathed from the dilemma.

Although the changes in the monarchy obviously caused the Earl some anxious moments, he does not appear to have been unduly disturbed by any religious implications.

The effect on his tenants was probably very different. The church was extremely important to the common people. It was not just a place they went to on Sundays; it was an inextricable part of their lives. They must have found the successive and often conflicting reforms which took place between the latter part of Henry VIII's reign and the accession of Queen Elizabeth both bewildering and incomprehensible.

We have no direct information concerning the effect of these events on the local community. However, thanks to the survival of the Dinton churchwardens' accounts for a period beginning in 1536, we have some clues as to what was taking place. Although the church they refer to is not Teffont but Dinton, Teffont Magna was of course still within its parish. One of the earliest accounts reveals a spat between Teffont and Dinton: an item of 2s was entered as the cost of a 'citation against the Inhabitants of Theffount'. However, the following year 20d bought a copy of a 'Composition between the Parishioners of Dinton and the Inhabitants of Theffount'. So it is to be hoped that the two communities were able to face the troubled years ahead in a spirit of amicability.

The early years' accounts indicate a flourishing church easily able to balance its books, thanks chiefly to profitable church ales and shepherds' suppers, helped out a bit by the sale of wool, the hiring out of its flock of sheep and the renting out of the 'church house' (the equivalent of today's village hall). The church ales were the great fund-raising events, held in the church house, which all the parishioners were expected to attend. They were not just drinking orgies; bread and cheese, and with a bit of luck, a dish of mutton from the church flock were offered. But then as now, the bar takings yielded the greatest profit.

The accounts for 1539-60 betray no consciousness of the dissolution of Shaftesbury Abbey, the institution which had held dominion over the parish for centuries past. It was business as usual so far as the church ales were concerned. All the same, it seems unlikely that the parishioners were not shocked to see the nuns—who styled themselves 'brides of Christ'—thrown out of their house as though they were common serfs. It seems improbable too that they would not have felt a shiver of apprehension.

In fact the rural churches were not gravely harassed during the remainder of Henry VIII's reign. There was a bit of tinkering with the services, and a ban on lighting candles before the statues of saints. (The accounts indicate less money spent on beeswax.) The greatest innovation was the requirement for an English version of the Bible—for which the churchwardens paid 5s 6d—to be put on display for all to see in the church. But the order was withdrawn a few years later, since it was deemed that 'women or the lower classes' were not fit to read the Testaments.

Far more ruthless changes were wrought after the accession of Edward VI in 1547. As the rampant reformers (among them the Duke of Somerset) gained the upper hand, orders were issued for the removal or destruction of virtually everything associated with Roman Catholicism. Chancel or rood screens, crucifixes, statues of the Virgin and the saints were all to be removed, chantries to be demolished, 'superstitious' stained glass to be replaced and wall-paintings to be white-washed over. Stone altars were to be replaced by more communicant-friendly wooden tables. Finally, the surrender of the church silver was demanded by the crown. It must have been a time of great anguish for the congregations of the parish churches, who were forced to stand by and watch the ornaments, often bought with their own hard-earned savings, so callously discarded.

Whether or not the Dinton church silver was confiscated is not indicated in the accounts. They noted, however, an item of 10d for the removal of the altar, 3s 9d for the purchase of lime and 6s 8d for 'washing the church'.

What may have been regarded as the unkindest cut of all was the banning of the church ales. For the parishioners it meant the loss of a rare opportunity for jollification, and for the churchwardens an obstacle in the way of balancing the books.

In 1553 Edward VI died, and the Catholic Queen Mary came to the throne. Orders were immediately given for the restoration of the Roman Catholic mass and wherever possible, the replacement in the churches of the sacred furnishings and icons. The Dinton churchwardens were obliged to pay 22d for two new altars (the authorities demanded a main and a side altar), but the church ales were allowed again, and in 1554 they raised the record sum of 32s 2d. One of the last legible entries in the accounts

Chancel screen in Teffont Magna church. (PL)

records the purchase of a new cope for the vicar, for the extravagant sum of 46s. The indications are that the Dinton/Teffont parishioners welcomed the return of the old faith.

Barely had the last plaster saint been patched up and restored to his or her niche, however, when Mary died, and the new queen, Elizabeth I, restored the Protestant faith. Fortunately the new regulations were not quite so arbitrary. The stone altar and images had to be thrown out once again, but Biblical texts, if not paintings, were permitted on the church walls. There was no ban imposed on church ales.

To what extent the Teffont churches were affected by these measures cannot be fully calculated. We may be happy that Teffont Magna was able to retain its delicately carved chancel screen. Of all the church furnishings destroyed during the Reformation, it is said that such screens were the most regretted by parishioners, for it had usually been they or their forebears who had raised the money for their construction. A fragment of stone bearing a consecration cross (preserved in the Teffont Magna church) is believed to be part of a medieval altar slab probably finally destroyed when Elizabeth came to the throne. There are also faint traces above the door of what may have been a Biblical text of the sort ordered to replace wall paintings.

There are unfortunately no surviving churchwardens' accounts relating to Teffont Ewyas. The only clues we have as to what happened emerged when the blocked up piscina in the church was discovered in the year 2000. Fragments of painted stone have been identified as belonging to at least one medieval shrine or altar, and slivers of stained glass as part of the original embellishment of an early window. Teffont Magna church's piscina may also have been blocked up, for at some stage it was damaged and its lobed base cut back to the level of the surrounding wall.

Teffont Ewyas had a new lord of the manor by the name of Henry Ley. When he acquired the manor in 1545 he was just a young man, with a tidy fortune and a new wife of good family: Dyonisia de St Maur (the original spelling of Seymour). When a young boy, his parents had died, leaving him a wealthy orphan. But he had come quite close to being deprived of his inheritance. He had been kidnapped by Sir Anthony Willoughby and imprisoned in Wardour Castle. Finally, after seven years, he had managed to escape, whereupon he married Dionysia, the daughter of his one-time guardian. Soon afterwards he sold the estate he had inherited in Devon and bought Teffont Ewyas from the Crown.

Fragment of stone bearing consecration cross. It is believed to be part of the original stone altar table in Teffont Magna church, destroyed during the Reformation.

He appears to have spent much of his life in arms, and was engaged in numerous battles, often under the auspices of Sir

William Pembroke. He obviously enjoyed royal patronage during the reign of Edward VI, and helped put down a rebellion in the west country against the introduction of the new Prayer Book. However, he managed to survive the revival of Roman Catholicism when Mary came to the throne. Like his patron William Pembroke, he showed an aptitude for negotiating the religious and political minefields of the 16th century. His rector, John Long, retained his position in Teffont Evias church from 1543 to 1555.

13th-century piscina in Teffont Evias church plastered over during the Reformation.

Henry Haucks served as rector of Dinton/Teffont Magna for much the same period. The task he shared with John Long—steering their churches through the tempestuous waters of the Reformation—was not an enviable one. It is impossible to know the religious convictions of either of them. At the time they were appointed there was still space for Catholics within the church. Even though there were some keen Protestants in the higher offices, the head of the church, King Henry VIII, despite his split with the Papacy, still regarded himself as a good Roman Catholic.

After King Henry's death, when under Edward VI the Protestants really came to power, any priest refusing to toe the line faced excommunication, or worse. It was a dilemma which faced thousands of conservative clerics throughout the country. Most of them decided to keep their dissent to themselves, and hoped the clouds would pass. Perhaps our two rectors were among them. The large outlay for a new cope as soon as the Catholic Queen Mary came to the throne suggests a certain enthusiasm in Henry Haucks for the old religion.

Teffont Magna church piscina, showing the base cut back. (PL)

One local parishioner who was not afraid to confess his adherence to Rome was Henry Mayhew. He was excommunicated as a result. When he died (in 1587) he was denied the right to be buried in the hallowed ground of Dinton cemetery, and was instead given a lonely grave in the unconsecrated churchyard of Teffont Magna.

The Mayhews were one of several Teffont Magna families, the

descendants of villeins or serfs, who had prospered. The latter part of the 16th century was a time of good harvests and increasing population, leading to a rise in the price of grain. For the poorer peasants unable to grow enough corn, it was disastrous; but for those who had surpluses it was very good news indeed. It brought them not only wealth, but also the possibility of increased status. The husbandman set his sights on becoming a yeoman, and the yeoman on becoming a member of the gentry. The Mayhew family had acquired at least the status of yeomen: they owned the freehold of a large tract of land in Dinton and Teffont. Despite the fact that Henry Mayhew's sons were exiled as a result of their father's religious convictions, the family retained the land until 1625. At the time of the sale it was described as 'the manor, lordship and capital messuage of Dinton and Teffont'.

William Mellowes was another upwardly mobile Teffont man who secured a 21-year lease of demesne lands in 1552. Another Teffont resident, John Rowden, was already prosperous enough in 1550 to make a will bequeathing 10 sheep, 3 bushels of grain and a bee-hive to six of his eight children. He even left the rector, Henry Haucks, a gift of 3s 4d.

There were losers as well as winners: if a man had not enough land to grow food to support his family, he had problems which could sometimes only be solved by becoming a labourer for his richer neighbour. However, there does not appear to have been any severe poverty in the parish. The churchwardens' accounts show only a few occasional pence paid out in support of the 'pore'.

The tenant farmers of Teffont Ewyas did not have quite the same opportunities for advancement as their neighbours in Teffont Magna, which was just a small corner of a vast estate; all the agricultural

The bleating gold of the chalklands.

land was leased, and the Earl of Pembroke, preoccupied with building his house in Wilton, was probably completely indifferent as to whether there were ten farmers with fifty acres, or one farmer with 500, so long as the rent was paid. By contrast, Teffont Ewyas was the only estate held by Henry Ley. He established himself there in the manor house, and he farmed a large area of the land himself. There was room for only one big fish in such a small manor.

Among the most important of the smaller fish in rural communities at this time were the shepherds. In Teffont Ewyas only one was necessary, for the few sheep owned by the tenants ran with the demesne flock of 300-400 sheep, and grazed the moderately fertile demesne land.

In Teffont Magna, however, it was a different matter. There were many more sheep owned by tenant farmers, and larger tracts of poor soil requiring fertilization. The sheep were therefore gathered into communal flocks and taken each morning onto the downland to graze under the supervision of the community shepherds. At the end of the day, the shepherds drove the flocks down to the valley again to be folded on the field selected—by means of a carefully drawn-up rota—for a night's manuring, penning them in with hurdles made from hazel wood. Since the time of sowing the fields varied according to which crop was being grown, the timing and positioning of the folds was crucial. Obviously a great deal depended on the zeal and competence of the shepherds. This was recognized by their above-average wages. They received enough to be able to hold their annual shepherds' suppers, through which they gave back money to support the community.

The importance of sheep in the local economy cannot be over-emphasized. They were mainly Wiltshire horned sheep, a sturdy breed which carried little fat, with long legs and light fleeces. Their meat, milk and cheese was therefore not of the highest quality, and was used mainly for local consumption, and their wool represented little more than the basis of a lucrative cottage industry. As a consequence, the farmers were not too much hurt by Edward VI's 'Relief of Sheep' poll-tax, imposing 8d per pound on the price of wool. Even when wool prices were at their highest, the corn crop was worth twice the value of the sheep products. However, without the sheep there would have been no corn to sell. For Wiltshire farmers in the 16th century —and for several more centuries to come-sheep were the bleating gold of the chalklands.

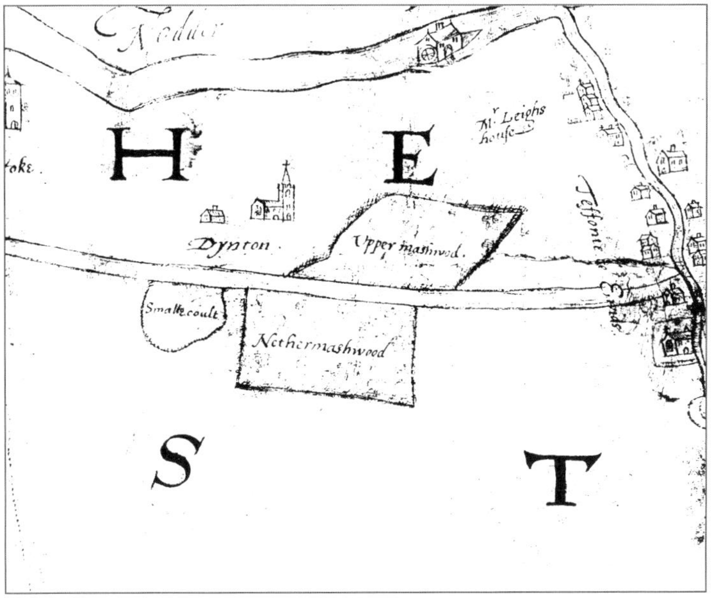

The earliest known map of this area (1589).
Reproduced with the permission of the Wiltshire Records Office

CHAPTER SEVEN

CIVIL WAR AND JOYLESS PEACE

Henry Ley died in 1574. There is a finely carved stone effigy of him in Teffont Evias church still retaining much of the original paint. He is wearing full armour of the Elizabethan period. His hands are not closed in prayer in the accustomed manner, but lie by his sides, his right hand within reach of his unsheathed sword; his shield rests on his left shoulder. He looks ready to spring up and defend himself. It may be that the pose reflects his attitude to life, which developed as a result of being kidnapped at an impressionable age.

The manor was inherited by Henry's son, William Ley. He had studied law, but 'by reason of infirmitie in his head' had retired to lead a quiet life in Teffont, where he rebuilt the manor house and kept an eye on his brothers. There is a bell in Teffont Evias church inscribed 'Mr William Ley 1611'. Presumably he presented it to the church, and very likely a second bell too, marked 'Feare God 1613'.

William died childless aged 80 in 1624, and was succeeded by his brother, Matthew, who had devoted most of his life to politics, and had represented Westbury in Parliament four times. But he was already 79 at the time of his inheritance, and he died without issue eight years later. There are stone effigies of the two brothers in the church, both clad in armour of the James I period, lying side by side on what is apparently a common tomb.

Matthew outlived his two younger brothers, John and James. John was the most adventurous of Henry Ley's sons. He too had studied law, but gave it up, not because of 'infirmities' in his head, but itchiness in his feet. He went to sea, and became a privateer, plundering Spanish ships, and went on to explore the lower reaches of the Amazon; he was probably the first Englishman to do so. But he never realized his chief ambition, which was to discover Eldorado.

James, the youngest son, was the most successful member of the Ley family. In 1569, when he was eighteen years old, his father had bestowed upon him the living of the church, very likely expecting him to take Holy Orders, as would befit a youngest son. But young James obviously had his sights on higher if worldlier things, and went to Oxford to study law. According to John Aubrey, the family butler conducted the services in his absence. However, since James Ley died before Aubrey was born, one should perhaps take his account of the matter with a pinch of salt. It seems more likely that a curate was appointed. At all events, James gave up the living in 1576 when he entered Lincoln's Inn, and perhaps no longer had need of the £60 per annum. From then on he steadily climbed the ladder of success. He was knighted in 1603 while attending the newly crowned king, James I, on a visit to Wilton House. He went on to become Chief Justice of Ireland, Lord High Treasurer and the first Earl of Marlborough. But he never became lord of the manor of Teffont Ewyas. It was his son, Henry, 2nd Earl of Marlborough, who inherited the manor on Matthew's death.

Bells of Teffont Evias church commemorating William Ley. (PL)

Henry's life was dull by comparison with his father's, and he gets barely a mention in any history book. One or two interesting facts emerge from his will, however. He gave instructions that he was to be buried 'in the new chapel at Teffont'. He left £10 for 'the new building of the seats in the body of the church', and added the intriguing words: 'God forgive her (Mary, his wife) those wronges shee hath done mee ... and those wronges I have done her'. It does not appear that his instructions were carried out; all we know is that his body was sent to Salisbury for a post-mortem. The Countess remarried shortly afterwards.

At the time James Ley was knighted in Wilton House in 1603, the head of the Pembroke household was the 3rd Earl, William Herbert. His father, Henry Herbert, the 2nd Earl, had already been dead for two years. Nevertheless, since he was Teffont Magna's overlord, he qualifies to have a little of his life recorded. He was an influential man and a trusted servant of Queen Elizabeth. He had even offered to raise an army of '300 horse and 500 foot' at the time of the Spanish Armada. But perhaps his greatest claim to fame was the fact that he married the beautiful but penniless sister of Sir Philip Sydney, and was Sir Philip's host at Wilton House when the poet's greatest works were written.

William Herbert, who succeeded to the title in 1601, clearly did not inherit his father's romantic disposition. Having used up a large amount of the Pembroke fortune while sowing youthful wild oats, he married Lady Mary Talbot, whose only attraction appears to have been her bank account. He is reputed not to have shown her great devotion. According to Lord Clarendon, he was 'immoderately given up to women'. However, Clarendon described the young man as being universally loved and esteemed.

The king, James I, certainly held William in high esteem. This is confirmed by the fact that the king

Effigies of Henry Ley and his sons William and Matthew in Teffont Evias church. Their noses were most probably hacked off by Parliamentarian soldiers. (PL)

was paying a visit to Wilton House when he knighted the young James Ley. William was subsequently appointed Lord Chamberlain, and he carried the crown at the coronation of Charles I.

Living as they did in an unpretentious outpost of the Pembroke empire, it is unlikely that the Teffont Magna farmers ever had any personal contact with their illustrious landlords. The Pembroke steward, however, would certainly have been a familiar face, and on the spot as soon as the rents fell due. He would also no doubt have been instrumental in drafting the Survey of the Manors of Dinton and Teffont in the years 1631-32.

This survey gives a detailed list of all the 'copy-hold' (leasehold) tenants in each of the two manors. It provides an interesting picture of Teffont Magna, as it was in the early 17th century.

It lists twelve families, each with between 50 and 100 acres of farmland. They had thatched, timber-framed houses containing at least two rooms; the houses were lofted, and sometimes had a second storey. Outside there was a 'backside' (a back yard), usually both a barn and a stable, a vegetable garden, and in some cases an orchard. Every farmer had a 'close' of meadow and arable land, and the right to pasture his stock on the common land. All the farmers held a few head of cattle and horses and—inevitably—large flocks of sheep (1,150 between them).

The wealthiest man in the village was 61-year-old William Baberstock, who held (copy-hold) 'a well-timbered dwelling-house with four rooms' valued at £25. The land upon which it stood later became the site of the Black Horse Inn. Several of the fields and pastures named among Baberstock's 65 acres —notably French Furze and Linterne—became attached to properties still existing in the village.

The Lay Subsidy Rolls of 1225 contained the name of an earlier Baberstock: Walter. He was one of the less well-endowed inhabitants of Teffont, with little more than a cow, a bullock and a load of oats to his name, and assessed at 4d. It appears, therefore, that although the Baberstock family had not travelled far during the preceding four centuries, they had certainly gone up in the world. It is evident from the will which William Baberstock left when he died in 1640 that he was not only a prosperous farmer, but a man of some refinement, for among his bequests were a number of books, silver spoons and a gilt salt-cellar.

The Pembroke survey recorded the state of all the houses, barns and stables of the tenants, which they were required to maintain in good repair. Failure to do so would result in fines being imposed upon them by the Manorial Court. Presided over by the landlord's steward, the court not only served the landlord but also settled local disputes between his tenants, as well as establishing rules for the cultivation of arable land, the regulation of grazing, and rights to timber. Rural officials were appointed by the court, including those stalwarts of the farming community: the shepherds.

John Aubrey wrote approvingly of the hard-working chalkland shepherds, whose 'flesh is hard, their bodies strong' and whose hard labour left them 'not leisure to read and contemplate of religion', comparing them favourably with the dairymen of North Wiltshire, who only milked cows and made cheese and fed mainly on 'milke meates, which cooles their braines ... and makes them melancholy, contemplative and malicious'.

A matter which would inevitably have been discussed at the Manorial Court in the early 1630s would have been the establishment of water meadows. Their purpose was to cover the ground with a thin sheet of running water, which deposited nourishing silt and at the same time kept frost at bay. The initial preparation was both costly and labour-intensive, for it required levelling out the fields bordering the river and then constructing a system of ditches and hatches to distribute the water, in addition to the employment of a special man, called a 'drowner', to manage them. But the result was certainly worth the effort, for it enabled a crop of grass to be grown in the early spring when the winter fodder was running out, and four times as much hay later in the year.

The development of water meadows represented the greatest agricultural improvement in the chalkland area in the 17th century. The idea appears to have begun on the River Piddle in Dorset at the beginning of the century. It was certainly in operation along the Wylye valley and in Chilmark by the 1630s, and the Pembroke survey reveals that William Baberstock had converted a 3-acre field adjoining the stream to the west of his farmhouse into a water-meadow some time before 1631.

William Herbert died in 1630 and was succeeded as the 4th Earl of Pembroke by his brother, Philip. Philip was handsome and generally well-esteemed, but he did have two rather serious failings: a foul mouth and a filthy temper. Nevertheless, he retained the King's favour, and became Lord Chamberlain like his brother before him. In 1641, however, his temper brought about his undoing. In the course of a quarrel he laid violent hands on the son of the Earl of Arundel. As a result the King sacked him from his position as Lord Chamberlain.

Later that year, the crisis which had been looming between the intransigent King and his defiant Parliament came to a head. Civil war looked increasingly certain, and the nobles of the land began to range themselves either behind the hereditary authority of the monarch or the constitutional rights of Parliament. Had it not been for his dismissal as Lord Chamberlain, Philip Pembroke would almost certainly have remained loyal to the King. As a result of the slight, however, he became an unlikely Parliamentarian.

At the other end of the village, in Teffont Ewyas, the lord of the manor was a Royalist. He was James Ley, 3rd Earl of Marlborough, who had succeeded his father in 1638. He was a sea-faring man, who had risen to the rank of Admiral.

Already in the spring of 1642 the Royalists and Parliamentarians were squaring up for battle, the leaders of each doing their best to raise an army. In the regions dependent upon the wool trade, which was suffering depression, there was a growing discontent with the King's government and a certain sympathy for the Parliamentarians. Nevertheless, the common people showed little enthusiasm for rallying behind either flag. This attitude was even more marked in the corn/wool-producing areas (which included the Teffonts), where the effects of the depression were less felt. The most willing recruits on both sides were drawn from the dregs of society, including convicted criminals.

War broke out in August 1642, and Philip, Earl of Pembroke, went into battle. He had been appointed the Parliamentarian general in the west. But soldiering was not his forte, and he was soon relieved of his command. The Royalist James Ley, Earl of Marlborough, had no more success as commander of a squadron of men o'war. But this was chiefly due to the fact that the King did not have any ships. The King did not have any money either, which may have accounted for the fact that in 1644 James Ley took out a mortgage for £1,000 on Teffont Ewyas manor.

Although Philip Pembroke did not distinguish himself on the field of battle, he was throughout the war an active back-room supporter of the Parliamentarians. Cynics suggested that the motive for his devotion to the cause was to secure the preservation of his beloved Wilton House.

Although most of the local farmers maintained an attitude of neutrality, it did not prevent them from being dragged into the war. Even if they escaped being pressed into service with one or other of the armies, they were frequently forced to provide billets for passing soldiers, and to allow their precious horses to be requisitioned.

Worst of all was the constant harassment and pillaging by ill-disciplined soldiers; as a result, the farmers were afraid to go to market or even sow seeds in their fields. Our villages had the misfortune to be within foraging range when Sir Edward Hungerford laid siege to Wardour Castle in 1642. His barbaric legions would not only take the last crust of bread from a village, but would also cause malicious damage to the fields if food was not forthcoming.

The villagers were happy when in 1643 the war moved away from Wiltshire, and the farmers were for a while able to harvest their crops and feed their families without harassment. But the tax collectors were never far away. They came from both the Royalists and the Parliamentarians, demanding a percentage from the impecunious farmers and imposing excise duties on their produce in order to finance their campaigns.

It was very probably the Parliamentarian solders who—out of exuberance and a sense of fun—hacked the noses off the Ley family effigies in Teffont Ewyas church.

On the other hand, it was not ignorant soldiers but the Parliamentary hierarchy who were in all likelihood responsible for the destruction of Teffont Magna's carved stone Saxon cross. There is no reason to suppose that until this time it was not still standing. However, an ordinance issued by the Lords and Commons on 28th August 1643 demanded 'the utter demolishing removing and taking away of all monuments of superstition or idolatry out of all churches chapels and open places before November 1643'. The churchwardens were given the task of demolition under penalty of 40s. The slashes across the two surviving fragments of the Saxon cross (see photograph on page 24) suggests that they carried out the order conscientiously; the cross's scroll decoration was sufficient to render it 'suspicious' and therefore subject to defacement. The missing pieces of the cross were very likely carved with figures the Puritans would have considered idolatrous, and therefore requiring total destruction.

In 1644 the war returned to Wiltshire with horrifying intensity. Wardour was again under siege, and there were bloody battles in Marlborough, Devizes, Warminster and Salisbury. The plundering was worse than ever: 'being so poor, and all the country store being eaten up, they have it not for themselves, much less for such cormorants', a diarist observed, referring to the starving peasants in the Salisbury district.

Some efforts were made to protect the land from marauders by an organization known as the Clubmen. Their aims were entirely apolitical: to defend their homes and property against whichever side threatened them. The Wiltshire leader was Thomas Benett from nearby Pyt House. But they were too ill-armed and weak to be effective. It was estimated that no more than one in twenty from the local farming communities joined his ranks. The last significant stand of the Wiltshire Clubmen took place at Broad Chalke on 1st July 1645, when they bravely demanded of Cromwell that the Wiltshire garrisons be placed under civilian control. His response was to call them 'poor silly creatures' and to take their leaders captive.

The war came to an end in 1646, with victory for the Parliamentarians. Now began the time for retribution. James Ley, Earl of Marlborough, was described as 'a delinquent in arms', and suffered the sequestration of his estate at Teffont Ewyas. But it did not slip entirely out of the Ley family's hands, since the tenancy was given jointly to Richard Fitz and William Ley (for the sum of £100 for one year, payable to the state).

Although there is no further mention of the name of William Ley, Walter Fitz, whose descendants were to become wealthy farmers in Teffont Magna, was in Teffont Ewyas in 1648. His name appears in a list entitled 'Monthly assessments for Relief of Ireland'—a tax raised to relieve the suffering of the Parliamentary soldiers in Ireland, whose 'backs were without cloaks and bellies without food'. Other names on the list include John Phipp, the vicar—at 10d one of the highest assessed –and Augustus

Hayter, first owner of the building which would become Howards House.

The man with the highest assessment—5s—was a Captain Ludlow. One suspects he may have been a relative of the powerful Parliamentarian commander, Colonel Ludlow, and was very likely occupying Teffont Ewyas manor. The money raised must have been diverted to some other cause, for it never did reach the starving soldiers in Ireland.

James Ley had turned his back on his native land, and with a party of adventurers had sailed out to the West Indies, where they attempted to colonize Santa Cruz. But their efforts failed—James was not one of fortune's favourites. Bad weather, ill health, and eventually Spaniards forced them to withdraw.

In Teffont Evias church hangs a coat of arms of Charles I dated 1635, one of the few arms of that period to survive in a parish church. It was found by Sir Edgar Keatinge in the loft of an outhouse at Howards House in1947, and it is thought likely that it was hidden there by James Ley to prevent it falling into Parliamentarian hands. The lozenge-shaped frame, usually denoting a hatchment—i.e. the arms of a deceased person—was occasionally, as in this instance, used to display royal arms. Its bad condition necessitated much restoration and repainting.

In 1649 Teffont Ewyas manor was—surprisingly—restored to James Ley by the Parliamentary regime, but almost immediately he set off again for the West Indies to make another attempt at colonization. In

Arms of King Charles I in Teffont Evias church (the hand bosses above represent the Mayne rebus symbol).

order to obtain permission from the Council of State in London, on a bond of £20,000 he had to undertake to attempt nothing against the government. This voyage apparently also ended in failure, for there are no reports of any successful colonization. Indeed, there are no reports of any happenings in James Ley's life during the next ten years, except that in 1652 he sold his estate to John Ashe of Freshford for the sum of £4,200.

There had been a number of changes in the recorded spelling of Teffont Ewyas throughout the previous century. On the deed of sale to John Ashe, however, it is written as Teffont Evias, and from that time onwards until today this spelling has generally been used. It will therefore be referred to by this name for the remainder of this history.

John Ashe, the new owner of Teffont Evias manor, was a man of substance from Freshford in Somerset, described as 'the greatest clothier in England' before the onset of the Civil War. A Presbyterian elder and Member of Parliament for Westbury, he devoted a great deal of both his time and his money to the Parliamentarian cause. After the war ended in 1646, he was appointed Chairman of the Committee for Compounding (the body set up to examine the rights of Royalists to retain their property), and as such would certainly have been aware of the sequestration of Teffont Evias. Having already viewed the property, therefore, he took the opportunity to buy it when it became available at an advantageous price in 1652. It was not the only estate he acquired. Amongst others, he had bought the manor of Beckington, Somerset in 1650. He was perhaps buying property to provide estates for his eleven children. He may have lived some of the time at Beckington, since both he and his wife are buried in the church there.

The reaction of the Teffont Evias tenants to their radical change of ownership from Church of England Royalist to Presbyterian Parliamentarian is nowhere recorded. It is possible that they were already converted. Non-conformity, with its emphasis on preaching from the Bible rather than the ritual of Communion, found wide favour among the country people. Although the rector, John Phipp, had been appointed by James Ley in 1638, the fact that he was retained by John Ashe indicates his acceptance of the Presbyterian service.

Teffont and Dinton remained a part of the Pembroke estate. In 1647 disaster struck their landlord: Wilton House was almost completely destroyed by fire. Devastating though it was, it at least provided Philip Pembroke with a distraction from his unenthusiastic career as a Parliamentarian. He threw himself into the rebuilding of his mansion, determined to make it even more glorious than before. Inigo Jones certainly advised him in the project, but it was the latter's assistant, John Webb, who was the actual architect.

It is perhaps fortunate that Philip Pembroke died early in 1650, for it was in that year that a law was passed making swearing a criminal offence, carrying, in the case of a baron, a penalty of 20s for each occasion. It could have been an expensive time for the maledictory Earl, had he lived.

Fines were imposed on a sliding scale. A commoner's oath would cost him 3s 4d—a sizeable chunk of his earnings. Nevertheless, the common people would probably have felt a growing need to vent their indignation, as the Puritan regime imposed ever greater restrictions. These included the banning of all sports and festivals (including Christmas), the wearing of ornaments, and almost any activity, including taking a walk, on the Sabbath. Many alehouses were closed, and village maypoles were chopped down.

Apologists for the Puritans point out that many of the festivals led to drunkenness, and that maypole dances were just a screen for licentious behaviour. So in banning them, the Puritans were acting for the welfare of the community. Closing the alehouses meant that the farmer took his meagre earnings home, and banning ornaments prevented his wife wasting pennies buying baubles from the visiting tinker. However, with even the simple pleasures of football or fives banned, there was no longer much fun to be had. The result was a growing nostalgia for the good old days of the kingdom, which sometimes led to rebellion.

One such rebellion took place in 1655 when Colonel Penruddock and a band of malcontents took over the city of Salisbury. He was soon ousted, and suffered the supreme penalty. But discontent was increasing. The Puritans were steadily losing their authority. Cromwell died in 1658, and by 1659, when John Ashe breathed his last, the Commonwealth was also in its death throes.

The Lodge, Teffont Evias, built as the gate lodge of the Manor House, 16th to 17th century.

CHAPTER EIGHT

FROM ASHES TO ASHES

Although John Ashe left his fortune divided among his seven sons, it was his son-in-law, Paul Methuen, who took over his business, and according to Aubrey, became the greatest clothier of his time. He founded Corsham Court, and John Ashe's portrait still hangs there.

It is surprising that John Ashe left the Teffont estate not to his eldest son, James, but to his second son, John. Later events suggest that James was not happy with this state of affairs, and may have contested the will.

In order to understand the bizarre situation which arose, it is necessary to jump forward 13 years to 1672, when John Ashe the second (the heir to the estate) came to make his will, not long before he died.

It emerges from this somewhat confused and petulantly written document that James, his brother, had forced him to sign a bond promising that if he (John) were to marry, he would pay his brother £500. James's motive for making this extraordinary demand was very likely to discourage John from marrying, so that on the latter's death the manor would come into his own or his heirs' possession.

What skulduggery was employed to persuade John to sign the contract is considerably less easy to fathom. There is a suggestion that he was in debt to his brother and—surprisingly—had inherited debts from his father. Also, as he states plainly in his will, he was afraid that his estate would be sequestered 'by reason of the greatness of my said brother's father-in-law, Sir James Harington'.

Sir James Harington had certainly been a big wheel in the Parliamentary hierarchy, but by the time John's father died, the Royalists were once again in the ascendancy. It may be that John was afraid he might get drawn into the retribution which Harington's 'greatness' might attract. Although Teffont Evias manor had been legally bought, the low price paid for it might have made it vulnerable to a Royalist sequestration bid.

But John's fears were not realized, and he had the last laugh. He reveals in his will that for years he had been secretly married to Elizabeth Foorsbroke, and he left behind not only a wife, but a healthy legitimate son. He left instructions to his executors to sell as much of his estates as necessary (he still

John Ashe of Freshford. *Courtesy of Methuen Collection, Corsham Court and Courtaulds Institute of Art*

owned land in Beckington and Westbury) in order to pay the £500 he had pledged to his brother, and also to settle debts and legacies inherited from his father.

It is surprising that John managed to keep his wife and son a secret. Admittedly he had spent a long period in Flanders, but according to his will he had returned to England and spent eight years with his wife in Teffont. He even planted a vineyard here. John Aubrey visited it and commented: 'Mr Jo. Ash of Teffont Ewyas has a pretty vineyard of about 6 acres made anno 1665'.

While John Ashe was keeping a low profile in Teffont, James Ley, Earl of Marlborough, the previous owner of Evias, was again sailing the seas. The newly restored King Charles II had appointed him commodore of a squadron with orders to sail to India to receive, on the King's behalf, the port of Bombay—a part of the dowry brought by the Queen, Catharine of Braganza. But the earl's habitual bad luck continued to dog him. The Portuguese governor refused to hand over the port, and James Ley was forced to sail home empty-handed. A couple of years later he was offered a plum appointment—Governor of Jamaica—but he was killed in a naval action against the Dutch before he was able to take it up.

The restoration of the monarchy was popular with the majority of the population, who were tired of the austere Puritan regime. There were some who were not content, however, especially non-conformist ministers, who were ordered to reintroduce the Anglican Communion in their churches. Among them was John Phipp, the long-standing vicar of Teffont Evias. He refused to obey the order, and as a result was deprived of the living. However, he appears to have retained his house in Teffont Evias and to have used it as a meeting place for Presbyterians. There is a memorial stone to his widow, Mary, who died in 1691 aged 80, in the Ley Chapel in Teffont Evias church, and John Phipp—very likely his son—is on record as the tenant of a sizeable plot of land in 1692. So it seems that the rector was not too harshly penalized as a result of his rebellion.

In 1650 Philip Herbert succeeded his father as the fifth Earl of Pembroke. One of his first actions was to divest himself of the Pembroke demesne land in Teffont Magna. It was cut off from his Dinton demesne and leased. It comprised 66 acres of arable land with a dwelling house, and the first lessee was John Rawlins. Later it was enlarged, and became known as Manor Farm. As such it continued to be farmed until it was split up in the last decade of the 20th century.

The leasing of the demesne estate represented a significant step in the course of development of Teffont Magna, which diverged so greatly from that of Teffont Evias. The latter contained a community increasingly dependent on a lord of the manor resident in the very centre of the village, holding much of its assets. By contrast, the wealth of Teffont Magna was divided up among an increasing number of yeoman farmers.

The difference was already demonstrated in the 'Relief of Ireland' lists of 1648 (referred to above) relating to the two villages. Apart from Captain Ludlow, there were only ten names on the Teffont Evias list, and only seven of these assessed at more than 1d. The Teffont Magna list contains twenty names, with eighteen paying more than 1d. The Daniell family, who had inherited the Baberstock estate through William's daughter, were at the top of the list (assessed at 2s 2d.).

Although Teffont Magna had been more or less cut out of the Pembroke estate, the earls still owned the land and remained the titular lords of the manor. Their history is therefore still of some relevance.

Philip Herbert, 5th Earl, was for many years a Parliamentarian M.P. Nevertheless, he found no difficulty in changing his spots when Charles II was restored to the throne in 1660. He even acted as cup-bearer at the King's coronation. Apart from that, he is chiefly noted for having sold the best pieces of the art collection so painstakingly acquired by his father. However, it is very possible that he was influenced by the sound of creditors beating their way to his door.

If this was the case, his situation would have been exacerbated by events which occurred in 1665. London was ravaged by the plague. Although, fortunately, most of Wiltshire escaped that scourge, it was assailed by another: the King. For several months the royal court took refuge in Salisbury. The honour of offering merely an evening's hospitality to His Majesty and his retinue at Wilton House could easily have cost the price of a major work of art.

For the Teffonts, however, the presence of the Court in the vicinity would not have been wholly bad news. The quantity of produce required daily for the royal table would have been prodigious. Even the meanest smallholder must have been presented with an opportunity to earn a few extra pennies.

Philip Herbert was succeeded by his son, William, in 1669. William led an uneventful life and died unmarried in 1674. As a result, his half-brother, Philip, became the 7th Earl—and the skeleton in the Pembroke cupboard. In the course of his—fortunately—short life (he died at the age of 20) he was accused at various times of blasphemy, violent behaviour, manslaughter and murder. He invariably managed to escape severe punishment, but became notorious for his barbarous behaviour.

His notoriety could not have failed to reach—and inflame—the ears of his tenants; if they committed offences a fraction of the gravity of his, they were dealt out harsh punishments by the Assizes.

The new lord of the manor of Teffont Evias was the eighteen-year-old son of John Ashe's secret marriage, John Ash Jr. (He appears to have dropped the 'e' from his name). As has already been noted, John's father left instructions for the sale of as much of his assets and property as was necessary to pay off his debts. The manor of Teffont Evias appears to have survived intact, but apart from that, all John Jr received was an income of £100 per annum. Consequently, although he suddenly found himself lord of all he surveyed, his outlook may have been clouded by the fact that he had been left almost penniless.

His situation may have been improved by his marriage that same year (1673) to Martha, of the family of William Jesse, who held some of the most desirable real estate in Chilmark, including two profitable quarries. Between the time of the marriage and Martha's death in about 1692, three children were born. Beyond that we know nothing of John Ash's life. It was a time of increasing hostility towards nonconformists, so a plan to renounce his heritage and seek a new life in America may have been gradually growing in his mind. Subsequent events demonstrate that he was a staunch Presbyterian, who did not lack the courage of his convictions.

Any feelings of discontent John Ash may have experienced could only have been exacerbated when Charles II was succeeded in 1685 by his brother, James II. His anxiety may well have spread through the Teffont community, since the King sought to re-impose the Roman Catholic mass. Even though the dissemination of information was limited, such was the alarm caused by King James's behaviour that ripples of it were felt throughout the kingdom. The prospect of civil war began to loom large. To the dismay of the local communities, among whom were some old enough to remember the miseries of the Cromwellian Civil War, the king led his army of 25,000 men to Salisbury and prepared to make a stand against the invading forces of William of Orange.

Sloop Point, the home of John Ash at Hamsptead, North Carolina—one of the oldest buildings in North America.

Fortunately King James finally admitted defeat. The army withdrew, and the strange Dutch king ascended the throne with James's Protestant daughter as his queen. Thus the threat of a return of Roman Catholicism was removed. But the approved religion was that of the Church of England, and dissenters, while they were not persecuted, were sometimes the object of discrimination.

Martha's death may well have brought John Ash to a decision. In 1692 he sold Teffont Evias to Christopher Mayne, and a few years later sailed for America. He took with him his second wife, Mary, and his children from both marriages. The family settled in Carolina, and acquired a cotton plantation near Charleston. John prospered, and soon rose to represent his county in the Carolina Assembly. Before long he was crossing swords with the Governor, James Moore.

The main subject of dispute was—ironically—religious discrimination. Even though the Charter establishing the Colony had specified that there would be complete religious toleration, an act had been passed by the Carolina Assembly requiring all members to take the sacrament of the Church of England. Infuriated by this flagrant abuse of power, John Ash agreed to lead a delegation to carry a petition to London, demanding the restitution of the Colonists' right to religious freedom. The petition was sympathetically received by the House of Lords and given the royal assent by Queen Anne in 1705. But John Ash never learnt of his triumph. He died in London in 1704.

For unknown reasons perhaps connected with his father's death, John Ash's eldest surviving son, another John, also returned to England and died here in 1711. His name is engraved on a Jesse family tomb in Chilmark churchyard. It is noted in the register that he was buried 'in wool', confirming that the parish had acted in accordance with the recently introduced law that shrouds should be made of wool (a measure designed to boost the wool industry).

John Ash's remaining offspring were to prosper. A great-grandson became Governor of North Carolina, and the town of Asheville in Carolina is named after descendants of the men who were once lords of the manor of Teffont Evias.

The connection between Teffont Evias and the Ashe family was re-established in the 1990s, when Tom Ashe Lockhart, a direct descendant of John Ash, paid a visit to his ancestral home. He subsequently became a regular visitor to the village and a generous benefactor of the church.

The Ashe family memorial, Hampstead, North Carolina.

CHAPTER NINE

NEW LANDLORDS AND A NEW ROAD

Christopher Mayne, the new lord of the manor of Teffont Evias, was another Devon man, from the village of Offwell, who in 1679 had married a Somerset girl: Mary Mompesson. This branch of the Mompessons was a highly respected and well-to-do family with property in different parts of Wessex, they were related to the prestigious owners of Mompesson House in Salisbury Cathedral Close. Mary received only £2,000 as a marriage settlement from her father, whereas Christopher's father contributed £6,000. The money was to be used for the purchase of land. It is surprising that Christopher Mayne proceeded to use £5,000 of the settlement to buy Mompesson's estate in Chicksgrove.

It is logical to suppose that Christopher and Mary went to live in Chicksgrove after their marriage, thereby becoming neighbours of John Ash. It is probable that they were already acquainted, since there was still a branch of the Ash family living not far from the Mayne establishment in Devon. Since there was no church in Chicksgrove, they very likely attended Teffont Evias church. Their son John was baptised there in 1688. When in 1692 John Ash decided to sell up and emigrate to America, Christopher Mayne obviously jumped at the chance to buy the manor, even though the asking price was £12,000 and there was apparently only £3,000 of his marriage settlement left.

The indenture (conveyance) covering the sale of the manor in 1692 reads more like a particularly complicated hire purchase agreement than a deed of sale. Christopher Mayne arranged to pay for the estate in three instalments: £2,000 down, then £2,000 after six months and a final £3000 before the end of the year. He further agreed to pay John Ash £400 per annum 'for 1,000 years' (i.e. for the remainder of his life) and to allow him the use of the manor. Presumably the matter was fully settled when Ash left for Carolina and the Mayne family took over Teffont Evias.

The 'Lease of Years' attached to the deed of sale of Teffont Evias is sufficiently comprehensive to give a detailed picture of the manor as it was at the end of the 17th century.

We gain the impression of a well-ordered landscape, with land carefully measured out, forming a

Christopher Mayne, died 1701.
Courtesy of W Keatinge

Mary Mompesson, wife of Christopher Mayne.
Courtesy of W Keatinge

Isabella, wife of John Mayne.
Courtesy of W Keatinge

John Mayne of Kensington, Isabella's son.
Courtesy of W Keatinge

patchwork of field and meadows. The demesne is dominated by the manor-house set in a park, with 50 acres of woodland and some 350 acres of agricultural land, the latter divided up into enclosed and named fields, but farmed by employees of the manor.

A further 200 acres or so is shared out, chiefly among tenant farmers, with acreages ranging from 6 to 75, each with its own farmhouse and outbuildings. It is extremely difficult to identify any of the farms, since they were not nucleated. Each consisted of a scattering of disconnected fields; this was a legacy, no doubt, from medieval times, when the peasant farmers were allocated non-contiguous strips of land, so that none should have a monopoly of the more fertile soil.

There is no mention of a vineyard. It may be that wine production was against John Ash's strict Presbyterian principles. That he took an interest in improving agricultural conditions on his estate is demonstrated by the fact that 21 acres of water meadow had been created, and 100 acres had been sown with sainfoin, a newly introduced type of grass used as animal fodder, which added some nutriment to the soil. Even when the land was leased to a tenant, the landlord still dictated what use it was to be put to.

There were two working quarries on the estate, one producing stone, the other tiles. Since few traces of 17th-century farm buildings remain, it is likely that many were still wattle-and-daub constructions. There were certainly some stone houses already standing (they are still in existence today), but they bear no identification marks of their original owners. There are two notable exceptions. One is the present Howards House, built in 1623 and bearing the initials of its original owner, Augustus Hayter: A E H. The other is Montague Cottage, which has a date-stone for 1682, with the initials of Ralph Montague. One of two 17th-century buildings nearby might have housed the estate bailiff. The first is a spacious cottage, now called Home Farm House; the second is the grand old rectory, which is known to have begun life as a farmhouse.

Edward Davis is recorded as leasing the largest farm in Teffont Evias (75 acres), and he had more land in Chicksgrove. He was the second of three generations of the same name to be buried in Teffont Evias church. As can be seen from their gravestones in the porch of the church, between them they clocked up 230 years. John Phipp—probably a descendant of the rector deprived of his living in 1662—held 34 acres. William Rowden very likely owed his eleven acres to the ten sheep and a bee-hive inherited by one of his forebears in 1550.

George Goodfellow was the miller. He was the second known tenant of the mill, having inherited the lease from his father in 1681. There may have been earlier unrecorded generations. There were certainly later ones until 1835. It is tempting to speculate that the name Goodfellow was derived from the miller being more trustworthy than his disreputable peers. There are Goodfellows living in our village today, but they are not sure if they can claim a direct descent from the millers.

Christopher Mayne was not permitted to enjoy being the lord of his new manor for long. He died in 1701 at the age of 46. His widow, Mary, managed the estate until their son John, who was aged 13 at the time of his father's death, was old enough to shoulder the burden. She also outlived her sister, with whom she was co-heiress to other Mompesson property. Mary brought her to be buried in the Ley Chapel, and erected the memorial stone for her, 'Dame Dinah Walrond', with her impressive coat of arms.

It is not known who erected the stone in the porch of the church commemorating Margaret Clos, described as the daughter of 'Monsieur Clos of Nyrenburg in the Palatinate'. How she came to die in 1680 in this remote Wiltshire village is a complete mystery.

The year after Christopher Mayne's death, 1702, William of Orange died and was succeeded by Queen Anne. It is unlikely that anyone living in Teffont Evias realized that the queen's favourite was a descendant of their previous landlords. The gentleman in question, who in 1704 was to become the victor of Blenheim and a national hero, was John Churchill, the Duke of Marlborough. He was a great-nephew of James Ley, 1st Earl of Marlborough, who had started his spectacular career as the negligent rector of Teffont Evias church.

Tapestry believed to have been begun by Isabella Mayne.

One of the trustees mentioned in the sale of the manor to Christopher Mayne was William Wyndham. A few years earlier he had bought the large estate comprising land in Dinton and Teffont, subsequently to be called Dinton Park. Since he was the son of the wealthy and influential Sir Wadham Wyndham, the purchase will have raised few eyebrows. Another land acquisition which might have caused more surprise was that of the not inconsiderable former demesne estate in Teffont Magna by Joseph Mould. Joseph Mould's father, who died in 1705, had leased a farm of a mere 32 acres on the Teffont Evias estate, but he also held the tile quarry, which perhaps accounted for the upturn in the family's fortunes. The land remained in the Mould family's hands until 1782, even though Jonathan Mould was brought before the Assizes in 1762, charged with 'running away and leaving his family chargeable to the parish'.

The Fitz family, whose ancestor Richard Fitz had leased Teffont Manor after its sequestration in 1646, had established a large farm in Teffont Magna and had already built a substantial stone house there in the 17th century. The profitability of the farm is indicated by the fact that in 1700 they added a new wing exclusively for the storage of the wool from their flocks.

Walter Baberstock's grand-daughter had married John Jesse, who had apparently taken advantage of the fact that his father owned the Chilmark stone quarries to rebuild the house. He left a date-stone to prove it—engraved 'J J M.1717'—over the front door. A stone in the wall of The Malt House, the grand old house adjacent to Teffont Magna church, previously called Bucks Close, bears the initials of John Hayter and the date 1795. It is known, however, that there was a building there a long time before that date.

The Pembroke Estate Survey meticulously recorded the annual rents payable by each of the tenant farmers. John Jesse paid the highest rate—£2—which does not sound outrageous, even by 17th- to 18th-century standards. But the tenant was obliged to pay a substantial amount for his lease, which was good for the holder and two successors. In addition there was a 'heriot' to pay when the holder died. It was usually one 'best beast', but occasionally as many as three. Although a long-established tradition, it seems a cruel penalty, forcing another painful parting on the bereaved—especially when the 'best beast' was likely to end up as mutton on the Earl of Pembroke's already groaning table.

From 1683 the 8th Earl, Thomas Herbert, was the master of Wilton House. Although a younger brother of the notorious Philip, he was described as a man 'of eminent virtue', and he carried the sword of justice at three successive coronations. His appointment as Lord High Admiral in 1701, however, caused some dismay among his peers and makes him appear a possible model for 'the ruler of the queen's navy' in Gilbert and Sullivan's 'H.M.S. Pinafore'. Not only had he never gone to sea; he had never even worn a naval uniform. He died in 1733 and was succeeded as 9th Earl by his son, Henry, known as 'the architect Earl'. He added a number of improvements to Wilton House, and amongst other things laid the foundation stone for Westminster Bridge. Like his father, it seems unlikely that he had anything to do with his tenants in Teffont, apart from occasionally eating one of their 'best beasts'.

By 1726 the manor of Teffont Evias had lost the second of its new line of lords: John Mayne died at the age of 38. His widow, Elizabeth, was the daughter of a wealthy merchant in Kensington. She was evidently a lady of fashion and refinement, with her own coach and personal maid. One gains the impression that rustic life did not greatly appeal to her. Nevertheless, she stayed on in Teffont to look after the estate until her son John Jr was old enough to assume the burden. It is said that she counted George Frederick Handel among her friends, and she may have had the occasional consolation of visiting him when he was staying with his friend John Harris in Salisbury.

Elizabeth died in 1768, leaving most of her property, including her Kensington house, to her daughter. To her son she left £400, a 'gold snuff-box cabinet', a tortoise-shell cabinet, the family portraits and his father's velvet mantle. She did not altogether forget 'the poor and indigent of Teffont'. She left them £10; but the poor of Kensington received £50. Elizabeth's heart may not have been in Teffont, but her body was buried there, close to her husband's, in the Ley Chapel.

John Mayne Jr appears to have inherited his mother's contempt for the countryside. Although he had been lord of Teffont Evias manor since the age of three, throughout his life he referred to himself as 'John Mayne of Kensington'. Little is known about his life beyond the fact that he 'sometimes practised at the Bar' and that at the age of 38 he married Isabella Raymond, a woman half his age. They had their portraits painted by Gainsborough.

It was the beginning of an unhappy period for the villagers of Teffont Evias. Not only did they have a landlord who remained aloof, but they were not even considered worthy of a rector. The previous incumbent, Thomas Mills, had retired (or died) in 1724. During the 54 years he had served as rector, great changes had taken place in the position of the country clergyman. He had risen in status from being little more than a servant of the squire to little less than his equal. Moreover, he expected to be given a comfortable rectory and a decent stipend. Thomas Mills may have put up with living in comparative penury, but it looks as though the Maynes had difficulty in finding someone to take his place. The subsequent two rectors, Jonathan Waterman, appointed in 1724, followed by John Bedwell in 1769, chose to reside in other parishes, where they already held offices, and to appoint humble curates to serve Teffont Evias church. By the 1780s the number of communicants there—even on high days—rarely exceeded a dozen.

John Mayne died in 1785. Since he left no children, the estate went to a distant cousin, Thomas Mayne. Apart from the family portraits, John Mayne left all his worldly goods to his wife.

It is surprising, given that he appeared to show little interest in them while he lived, that John Mayne left a bequest of £100 for the poor of the parish—a large sum, by 18th-century standards. It suggests that there was large-scale poverty in the village. It was indeed a time of increasing hardship for the Wiltshire farming communities, mainly due to poor harvests. The landless were especially badly hit, since the price of corn had risen, but not the wages of a farm labourer. As a single man, lodged on the farm, the labourer could manage, but, once married, his lot was very likely a rude hovel on an unproductive piece of ground, with barely enough money to feed his family. Unlike during the 16th century, there was no opportunity for his wife to supplement the family income by spinning or weaving. The fortunes of the partly-mechanised Salisbury cloth industry fluctuated, but there were so many unemployed spinners and weavers in the city that even during boom years, there was no work available for the villages. One of the few profitable activities left for the farm-worker's wife was to collect hazel nuts in the woods.

John Mayne's widow, Isabella, soon found a second husband—an aristocrat, to boot. But the 9th Earl of Dundonald proved to be both eccentric and a spendthrift. Having spent all the money he could squeeze out of his wife, he went off to Paris and died there in poverty. Isobella lived out the rest of her life in her natal home in Belchamp, and left all that remained of her fortune to her brother.

Meanwhile Thomas Mayne had taken possession of Teffont Evias manor. He lived for only two years, but by the time of his death in 1787 he succeeded in completely breaking up the estate. Bequests, including £7000 to his daughter Mary, would necessitate the sale of almost all the Mayne property with the exception of Teffont Evias—and still leave his son in debt.

The quality of life for the working people of Teffont Magna had been improved by an unexpected turn of events. In 1756 the road from Salisbury to Mere, from which there was access to Exeter and other towns of the south west, was upgraded to a turnpike, chiefly for the benefit of the ever-increasing coaching traffic. It is not hard to imagine the Teffont inhabitants watching with bemusement and perhaps some scorn the coach-loads of gentry as they rattled by. Then one day it occurred to a widow called Grace Mullens (or Daw) that there was a way of making a profit out of the coaches. She had inherited a 'decayed cottage and stable adjoining' from her father, and out of this she created the Black Horse, a friendly inn where the travellers could refresh themselves and rest their rattled bones. Standing at the ten-mile mark out of Salisbury, it became the recognised point for the first changing of horses and a stopping place for the mail-coach.

There will doubtless have been a number of others in the village who were able to profit from the turnpike: brewers, bakers, blacksmiths, farriers, stable boys and perhaps even wheelwrights. There would also have been a requirement for men to do maintenance on the road. Not a particularly attractive proposition perhaps, but no harder than labouring on a farm and perhaps better paid.

There was, of course, a downside. Local farmers were not immune from paying road tolls, and there were toll gates at both Chilmark and Wilton. The rates were high: 10d for a score of cattle and 5d for a score of sheep. A wagon with 2 horses cost 3d, only half the price of a 2-horse coach. Even a single horse was rated at 1d. There were riots in some parts of the country when turnpikes were first introduced. However, it is hard to believe that our local farmers, who would have known the country like the backs of their gnarled hands, would not have been canny enough to find ways of avoiding the toll gates. The ox-drove became a well-known alternative route.

In the year 1778 the turnpike will have provided an interesting spectacle for the inhabitants of Teffont Magna.

By this time their landlord was Henry Herbert, 10th Earl of Pembroke. A few years earlier he had stirred up a great scandal by abandoning his Countess and his position at Court, and running away with Kitty Hunter, the wayward daughter of one of the Admiralty lords. But his faux pas had by now been forgiven (if not forgotten), and the king and queen were about to demonstrate that he was back in favour by paying him a visit. But the Earl had a problem: although there was no shortage of elegant bedrooms in Wilton House, he lacked a king-sized bed. It was well known, however, that William Beckford Sr, the master of Fonthill Mansion, had had one made for his state bedroom, and the Earl arranged to borrow it. It was therefore slung on a wagon and transported along the turnpike from Fonthill to Wilton. One can imagine the Teffont residents staring with disbelief as it trundled through the village.

They were no doubt familiar with the sight of the ostentatious Beckfords, father and son, travelling along the turnpike with their retinue of liveried coaches and outriders.

They may even have enjoyed their hospitality. One such opportunity occurred in 1797, when to celebrate the completion of his house, William Beckford Jr threw a Twelfth Night party. He invited not only the local gentry to it, but also 11,000 local peasants. Our Teffont peasantry may not have had the necessary credentials to have been among the lucky 700 given a sit-down dinner of roast meat, but they would almost certainly have been among the remaining thousands who were all provided with bread, beer and a variety of entertainment.

It must have provided a welcome break from the cold and misery of January, when food stored in the autumn might be running out. Was it the hunger caused by a bitter winter in 1785 which drove James Butt to steal a sheep from Oliver Smith's farm in Teffont Magna? Whatever the reason, his punishment was transportation.

At least by this time the majority of the villagers of both Teffonts had stone houses in which to shelter from the rigours of winter. Their thick walls and thatched roofs provided some insulation from the cold. But what made them habitable (although not necessarily comfortable) during the bitter winter months was that feature considered today so charming in old cottages: the inglenook fireplace. For the 18th-century cottage family, it would have been the mainstay of their lives. During the cold, dark winter days, it provided light as well as warmth; they would have cooked on it, dried their clothes by it and baked their bread in the adjoining oven. A disadvantage was that it was liable to fill the room with smoke. But where there is smoke there is fire. The great fear of the family huddled up before it must have been that they would not have enough fuel to keep it going through the winter.

Spring Cottage (left) and Edmeads Cottage (right).

Hope Cottage, with Fitz House in distance.

Riverside Cottage.

Rose Cottage.

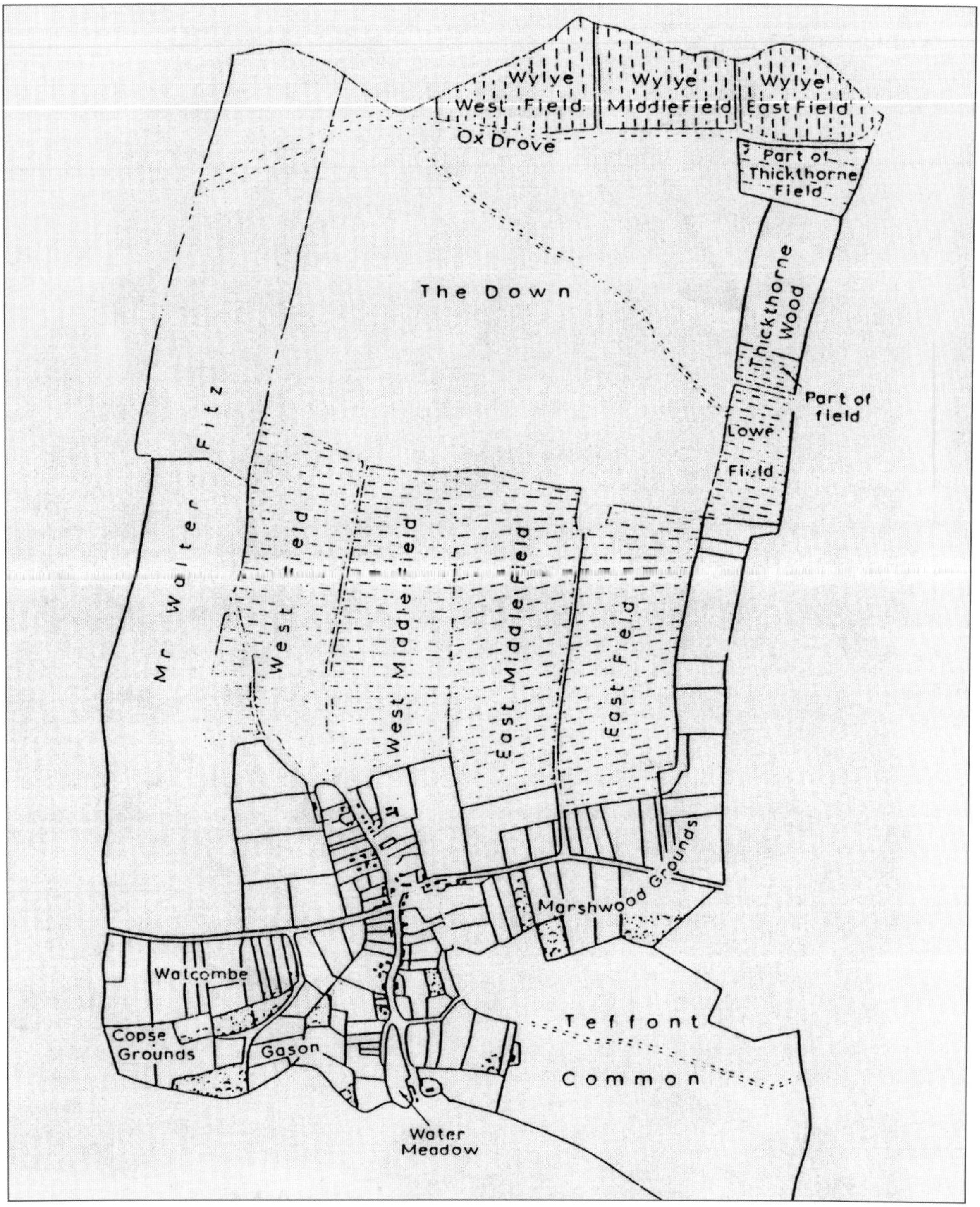

Teffont Magna parish, 1801. Based on a map made for Lord Pembroke by John Charlton.
Courtesy of Victoria County History

CHAPTER TEN

MAINLY THE MAYNES

When In 1787 Thomas Mayne Jr, under the terms of his father's will, became lord of the manors of Teffont Evias and Chicksgrove, as well as the owner of considerable land in Devon, it is unlikely that he realized that he had been handed a poisoned chalice. A miniature portrait, probably painted a few years earlier, gives the impression of a shy, amiable young man, with neither great ambition nor sharp wits.

This is conjecture; what is certain is that he was totally unfitted to deal with the problems which were thrust upon him by his father's will. These, to put it in a nutshell, placed him under the obligation to settle debts and pay out large legacies with no liquid assets to draw on. His situation was made even worse by the fact that he inherited a crooked lawyer, named Charles Lucas, attached to the will as a trustee. As a result of bad, sometimes dishonest advice, he hastened to sell off his Devon estates at Ottery St Mary and Honington, as well as valuable land in the city of Exeter, accepting far less for them than their true value. Two farms on the Chicksgrove estate were picked up at a bargain price by a Mr Moody.

But Thomas was still unable to discharge all his debts, and his creditors—grocers and chandlers, as well as his sister Mary Wrench and her husband—continually harassed him. Thomas's uncle, William Stalker, described the latter's behaviour as 'unparalleled acts of villainy and deceit'. In 1790 Thomas wrote in a letter to his uncle how desperately he hoped 'some method may be found to lighten the burden under which I have been sinking these three years'. He was unable to sell any part of Teffont Evias manor because it had only been left to him in trust. He did succeed in raising £1,000 by selling oak trees from the estate. (Oak was in great demand for the building of battle-ships in anticipation of war with the French.) But they bought him little more than a stay of execution. There was still not enough left in the kitty to settle all his debts, and his creditors—including his sister—pressed him harder than ever. As a consequence, in 1792 Thomas Mayne found himself in a debtors' prison.

He was sent, not to the notorious Fleet or Marshalsea prisons, but to the King's Bench in Surrey. It was a slightly more debtor-friendly establishment than the former two, but still not the sort of place in

Margaret, wife of Thomas Mayne. *Courtesy of W Keatinge* (VK)

Mary Wrench, sister of Thomas Mayne. *Courtesy of W Keatinge* (VK)

John Thomas Mayne. *Courtesy of W Keatinge* (VK)

Sarah, wife of John T Mayne, with their children—Augustus (left), Emily (right), and Margaret (on Sarah's lap). *Courtesy of W Keatinge* (VK)

which you would expect a loving sister to cause her brother to be confined. Fortunately a law was enacted in 1794, under which in certain circumstances debtors could be released. In order to obtain his release, Thomas was obliged to convey his entire property to the Clerk of the Peace for Surrey, who assigned it to three of his principal creditors, a grocer, a wine-merchant and an upholsterer, making them trustees of the estate. In 1802 it was sold by public auction; the creditors were paid off, and Thomas was allowed to keep the change, amounting to £566 3s 2d.

One can only guess at the effect these events will have had on the tenant farmers of Teffont Evias. They were no doubt aghast to learn that their lord had been thrown into a gaol for debtors, and probably fearful in case their leases were in jeopardy. However, so far as one can gather, they were left to carry on their business as usual, even though for a while they found their farms to be the property of a trio of tradesmen. The notice for the 1802 auction-sale specifies that it included farms occupied by George Macey, Henry Larkham and John Goodfellow.

Mr Wyndham bought Thomas Mayne's life interest in Teffont Evias. Thomas's wife, Margaret, and the child who had been born the year his father went to prison, moved back into Teffont Manor soon after 1802, presumably as tenants of the Wyndhams. But Thomas did not join them until shortly before his death. A serious rift had obviously developed between Margaret and her husband. This may have been due to disappointment on his part over lack of support from her. (It has even been suggested that she took her sister-in-law's part.) On the other hand, she may have felt let down by not receiving the financial support to which she felt entitled.

The situation had been exacerbated by the fact that Thomas was (shhh!) a Dissenter. It was a matter which caused his son great embarrassment in later years. Thomas's sister had also been brought up as a Dissenter, but she had been baptised in Teffont Evias church in 1789. It is perhaps significant that during the last year of his life, when Thomas returned to his family in Teffont Evias, he too was baptised.

The new landlord of Teffont Magna, George Herbert, who succeeded his father to become 11th Earl of Pembroke in 1794, had something in common with Thomas Mayne. He also had been left ill-provided for by his father. Even though Henry Herbert had returned home and toed the line after his scandalous affair with Kitty Hunter, he had further love affairs, became an inveterate traveller, a serious collector of objets d'art and in every sense a bon viveur. As a result, he left the coffers of Wilton House fairly empty. He had done his utmost to persuade his son and heir to marry a rich wife, but George Herbert had insisted on marrying his pretty but penniless cousin, Elizabeth.

George Herbert's poverty, however, was not in the same league as Thomas Mayne's. Somehow or other he managed to raise £200,000 which he used to restore Wilton House (with the help of James Wyatt), and to undertake major improvements to the estate, and as a result he was able to increase his rent-roll from about £35,000 per annum to over £100,000.

In 1793 the French Revolutionary Government declared war on Britain. As a result of the emergence of daily newspapers, people at home in England could follow the war's progress. News of events would even have reached Teffont, since the mail-coach would doubtless have delivered a copy or two of the Daily Universal Register (the forerunner of The Times) at the Black Horse. Not many of the villagers would have had the means to read it, let alone buy it, but news of Nelson's great victories would most certainly have been passed around. Consequently, when in 1801 Nelson passed through the village on his way to Fonthill to visit William Beckford, the local people—like the rest of the British populace—will no doubt have lined the road to watch his coach pass. They may have had the added excitement of catching a glimpse of the notorious Lady Hamilton.

For most of the agrarian farmers, the Napoleonic Wars, which started in earnest in 1803, came as a shot in the arm. Until the outbreak of hostilities, grain was being imported to help meet the demands of the growing urban communities. Blockading by the French, however, interrupted the supply. As a consequence the local farmers could now profitably sell as much corn as they could grow.

In order to increase grain production, more land had to be cultivated and ways found of improving the yield. The early 19th century witnessed great changes in farming methods. It was not only the Earl of Pembroke who invested money in improving his land. Throughout the country there was a great surge of land improvement. It was brought about by the use of more efficient tools, the consolidation of land, the introduction of new crops, the extension of water meadows and above all by enclosure. In Teffont Magna, the common, Upper East and Lower Field were among the pieces of land enclosed in 1837.

An entirely different type of farming developed, based not on self-sufficiency, but on sale potential. There was no longer a place for the smallholder, or even a small-scale farmer tending parcels of land in different locations. They were gradually squeezed out as their larger neighbours took possession of the total area of the fields—often including bits regarded as common land—and planted hedges around them. The farmers who climbed to the top of the heap in Teffont Magna appear to have been Walter Fitz, Edward Mould, William Macey, Edward Larkham and Oliver Smith. Their pecking order was established by the allocation of pews in the church.

The high price of corn certainly enabled the bigger farmers to feather their nests, but it was not so beneficial for the rest of society. Bread was the staple food throughout the land, and its price rocketed. The inflationary trend is even reflected in the quarterly bills for the Communion bread and wine submitted by the Teffont Magna church wardens: these rose steadily from 1s 10d in 1787 to 2s 8d in 1805 and 3s 6d in 1814, even though the number of communicants did not increase.

Although it was still a chapel of ease, Teffont Magna church was in most respects independent from Dinton. Regular services, including Holy Communion and baptisms, were being conducted within its walls. Rates for its maintenance were fixed annually by its own Vestry and levied from its parishioners. The only rite it was denied was that of burial, and its dead had to be carried on a bier along the coffin trail, which ran through the woods by the side of the road to the cemetery at Dinton.

In addition to the rates, the church's only other source of income was the Chapel Hall. Like today's village hall, it was rented out for local functions. Sunday schools for the village children—which churches were being encouraged to provide—would also have been held there.

Churchwardens were appointed annually from among the principal farmers. This appointment may have been regarded as a penalty, for the post was no sinecure. Among the warden's duties was the preparation of a 'presentment' for the annual 'Visitation' of the Archdeacon of the diocese. This was a detailed report on the state of the fabric of the church and the behaviour of the parishioners. Every irregularity, from whoredom and drunkenness to the untimely ringing of bells had to be listed, and the warden could be charged with perjury if he recorded anything incorrectly. Such 'Visitations' proved expensive (sometimes as much as £1 a time), for in addition to other charges the august visitors expected to receive hospitality—a lunch at the Black Horse, perhaps.

Within the rates administered by the churchwardens was a special fund for the destruction of vermin. A variety of creatures, including hedgehogs, came under this heading. 'Sparrows' heads' accounted for the biggest drain on the budget: money was paid for the destruction of seed-eating birds, usually by the farm-workers' children. In 1819 a total of 19s 6d was paid out (representing about 700 birds). Only the heads were demanded. The bodies were eaten, usually roasted over a fire.

The inflated price of corn was disastrous for the poor. Farm labourers' wages in the chalklands remained pitifully low. Between 1794 and 1842, apart from a brief period around 1804, they did not rise above 8s. per week, and many were reduced to eating potatoes grown on their own small patches of land in place of the bread they were accustomed to eating.

In 1810 the farm labourers of Teffont Evias were struck by a terrible calamity. The thatched roofs of the cottages had always made them a fire risk, and over the course of the years more than a few had been burnt down. On this occasion, however, a spark from the chimney of the bakery started a conflagration which destroyed eight cottages. There was apparently no loss of life, but the inhabitants no doubt lost their few miserable possessions.

Shortly after 1800, a decision had been taken to reroute the turnpike, so that it ran along the course of today's B3089. This will have been devastating news for William Seagrim, the lessee of the Black Horse, who would be left with a coaching inn on an empty road. Edward Larkham may not have welcomed the project either, since the route of the new road ran straight through the middle of his farm. But some time may have elapsed before the road was constructed. When Seagrim's lease was sold in 1827, the property was still described as being in a 'situation very desirable for a Posting House, with convenient Dining and other rooms, Brew House, Cellars and offices'. It looks as though the buyer would have been well advised to conduct a search! Larkham's Farm was eventually converted into a posting-house and took over the name of the Black Horse, but it was not until 1843 that reference was made to it as an inn, with Mary Ann Shergold as inn-keeper. The old inn is still there today, converted into a comfortable dwelling-house, with the name Black Horse Cottage.

About the same time as the opening of the new Black Horse, an establishment of a different character opened its doors a few hundred yards away: a Methodist Mission House. It was a modest building scarcely distinguishable from the surrounding cottages, but in its heyday it attracted a large congregation from both Teffont and Dinton, chiefly from the working community. The services were austere, and often included chastening sermons delivered by lay preachers. The chapel had little attraction for those who aspired to having their own pew—or their own beer-mug in the Black Horse, for that matter.

The most important family in the parish were the Wyndhams. Indeed, they considered themselves socially equal if not superior to the Maynes. Although Wyndham's land was mainly in Dinton, his authority was certainly felt in Teffont Magna. When in 1830 the blacksmith's dog mauled a child and then died of what looked like rabies, it was Wyndham who took charge of the situation. He gave instructions that all the dogs in the village should be destroyed—extreme measures, perhaps, but at that time the only certain method of containing the dreaded disease.

William's late father had been a good friend to the unfortunate Thomas Mayne, and William now offered his friendship and advice to the Maynes' young son, John Thomas, who was a very different character from his amiable but ineffectual father. He was a ruthless dynamo, with nothing but contempt for his luckless parent.

From an early age he demonstrated his determination to recover his family's property, and he began cleaning up the churchyard and planting trees long before he had regained possession of the land. He succeeded in getting the manor back in 1813, the year when he became twenty-one. He found means of raising £3,000, and bought back his father's life interest from Wyndham. He did not, however, have the money to offer his tenants the roast ox and barrel of strong beer which he had intended, to celebrate his birthday; 'circumstances not yet allowing of my exercising any spirit of liberality', he wrote. Instead he distributed a dozen Bibles and testaments among them.

His next move was to take out a mortgage for £10,000. He was to use this money to make improvements to the house, the church and the estate. However, he put some of it to immediate use, financing the last two years of his legal training—a precaution against being taken to the cleaners by rascally lawyers, as his father had been.

His aim was to pay off his debts by making an advantageous marriage. 'A decent person, of good temper, accomplished manners and a tolerably heavy purse' was the sort of lady he had in mind. His chosen bride, Sarah Fulcher-Start, was the daughter of an apparently wealthy man, and brought with her the promise of an inheritance of £20,000. A somewhat macabre explanation for his good fortune may be that Sarah suffered from erysipelas, an exceedingly painful and unsightly skin disease (also known as St. Anthony's fire.) As a result, her family may have had difficulty in arranging a desirable match for her. When Sarah's father died, however, it emerged that his funds fell short of the £20,000 that he had promised Sarah. The extent of John Mayne's disappointment and fury can only be imagined. Fortunately Sarah's elder brother undertook to make up the amount from the legacy he was confident of receiving on his mother's death.

Despite her ill health, Sarah gave birth to seven children, although three of them died at or soon after birth as a result of inheriting erysipelas. In addition to losing a baby in 1826, she also lost her beloved younger sister. The 13-year-old Mary Anna Start sickened and died while staying at the manor. There is a plaque to her memory in Teffont Evias church. Sarah's sufferings are often mentioned in the diary of Frances Lear, wife of the rector of Chilmark, who befriended the unhappy young mother. She also commented on the disagreeable nature of Sarah's husband. For John Mayne the death of his sister-in-law was not entirely bad news, for she had left a legacy of £15,000, some of which is thought to have found its way into his pocket. It was certainly an opportune time for a windfall to drop into John Mayne's hands, since even though he was unable to pay off his mortgage, he had embarked on a formidable programme of improvements to the estate. He began his absorption of leased farmland into the Manor Farm, so that by 1840 his acreage had increased from 140 to 348 acres. He embarked on the conversion of the fairly modest house he had inherited into a residence fit for a gentleman. He extended it, and built on a third storey topped with embattled parapets; he added towers and Gothic porches. He must have been delighted with the engraving produced by S.Rawle in 1821 which bears the caption:

Teffont Evias Manor House
To John Thomas Mayne Esq, F.R.S. F.S.A. His seat

John Thomas Mayne then turned his attention to upgrading the unpretentious medieval church. He engaged the architect Charles Fowler, and succeeded in persuading friends to contribute towards the substantial costs. The church which emerged was taller, with a pinnacled roof, an added aisle on the north side incorporating the 15th-century side-chapel, and an elegant two-stage tower to replace the former simple belfry. The Hanoverian royal arms, dated 1820, carved in stone by J.C. Bubb, were placed on the southern wall above the entrance. The rebuilding was completed in 1824, but a few years later a

Teffont Ewyas church, before rebuilding by John T Mayne.

Teffont Evias church, after rebuilding by John T Mayne.

budding young architect, George Gilbert Scott, added a third stage and a graceful spire to the tower.

The newly restored church was obviously kept spick-and-span, for over the next few years the churchwardens were paying as much as 5s a year for brooms and mops—articles which can only have cost a few pence each.

In 1830 the peace of the neighbourhood was disturbed by the Swing riots. The name 'Swing' was that of a fictitious captain who was supposed to be leading the riots. His followers, however, were real enough: poor, desperate farm labourers. The cessation of the Napoleonic wars had brought an end to the agricultural boom and the high price of corn. This sounds like good news for the landless, but it was swiftly followed by a severe recession resulting in the lowering of farm wages to 7s per week, and the laying off of farm labourers, so they found themselves worse off than ever. William Cobbett observed in 1825 that he had never seen such misery among labouring people as those in Wiltshire.

For these miserable farm-workers the introduction of new, steam-powered farm machinery proved to be the last straw—especially the threshing machines, which the labourers suspected would take away the little work available during the winter. So they went on the rampage, burning ricks and smashing machinery.

There was apparently no trouble in either of the Teffonts. (Wyndham had taken the precaution of swearing in a constable.) But some local villagers supported the rioters on other estates, and got arrested for their pains. Two such men were Jack Ford of Teffont Magna and Edmund White, probably of Chicksgrove, both of whom were sentenced to transportation to Australia. William Wyndham tried hard to get Edmund White's sentence mitigated, since he was reputed to be an honest, hard-working blacksmith, who had been led astray. He had no sympathy for Ford, however, who was a notorious poacher. Jem Larkin, another Teffont

The interior of Teffont Evias church, as designed by John T Mayne. (VK)

man, was transported a few months later for the crime of stealing grain.

In 1831 John Mayne appointed a new rector. His choice was Samuel Broomshead Ward, a man of good breeding and with a keen sense of his own importance. A few months after moving into the house designated as his rectory he set about landscaping the garden. He diverted the stream from its natural course on the east side of the road so that it ran through his garden, and dammed it to form a pond and waterfalls. A few years later he had the house extended by adding a new wing designed by George Gilbert Scott. One thing which the newly restored church lacked was heating. Ward rectified this to the extent of installing a stove in the chancel, close to the pulpit. Coal was provided out of the church funds.

In 1832 John T Mayne stood for parliament for the constituency of Chippenham, provoking some caustic comments from the Wyndhams. They were particularly derisive over his claim that his workers were especially well cared for, whereas—so Wyndham asserted—they were constantly complaining about the hard-heartedness of their landlord.

Mayne was not successful; so he set off in a coach-and-four to take his family on a grand tour of Europe. While in Holland he bought a number of fine pieces of medieval stained glass. These were discovered many years later and fitted into the windows of Teffont Evias church, to charming effect. He was very impressed with Switzerland, and when rebuilding The Cottage (later to become Howard's House), he designed the roof in the style of a Swiss chalet.

During his absence, he had leased the manor house to the Hon. Grantley Berkely, whom some of his

The Reverend Samuel Ward's rectory, with the additional wing designed by George Gilbert Scott.

neighbours found even more disagreeable than his landlord. He took great pleasure in shooting: he boasted of killing 700 head of game in 6 days. But according to Frances Lear, he had a distinct aversion to paying his bills with the local tradesmen. On his return, Mayne quarrelled violently with him. It was even rumoured that they fought a duel. In any event, Grantley Berkely departed, and John Mayne moved back into his house.

Window with medieval Dutch glass inserts.

Grantley Berkely was by no means the only person with whom Mayne crossed swords. Indeed, he appears to have fallen out with almost everyone around him at one time or another, including his family, his rector and his old friends (notably William Wyndham). The latter's aunt, Ella Wyndham, observed in a letter that John Mayne was 'certainly not in his right mind'.

However, from what we have learned of his life, Mayne appears not so much unhinged as obsessed. His early years were almost completely devoted to restoring his family's property and acquiring prestige. The older he grew, the more obsessed he became with the idea of glorifying the name of Mayne. This is demonstrated in Teffont Evias church, where there are numerous reminders of the Mayne family: tablets, coats of arms, and the Mayne rebus emblem, an open hand (from the French 'main', meaning 'hand') in the form of bosses in a band below the ceiling. It appears that he even changed the family name engraved on the tombstone of Dionysia to St Mayne, in order to suggest links with the Ley family.

His last years were not happy ones. In 1840 there was a tremendous storm, as a result of which the church, his pride and joy, was flooded 'being such as never before remembered'. It cost more than £3 to clean it out. Having finally after years of quarrelling reached an understanding with his only son, Augustus, he saw the boy die of scarlatina in 1841. Thus, ironically, after doing so much to enhance the prestige of the name of Mayne, there would be no-one left to bear it after his own death.

Two years later John T Mayne died. His memorial reads:

'During a long period of years he watched with anxious solicitude over the interest of the parish and it

John T Mayne's coat of arms. (PL)

was through his instrumentality that the church was rebuilt and the tower re-erected with the addition of the beautiful spire'.

These days the rebuilding of the church is largely regarded as a matter for some regret. However, in John T Mayne's time, the Gothicization of a rustic country church was seen as pleasing to both men and God. What is entirely uncontroversial among his achievements is the restoration of the Mayne family fortunes, which by his dogged endeavour he rescued from the brink of disaster.

CHAPTER ELEVEN

THE RICH MAN IN HIS CASTLE, THE POOR MAN AT HIS GATE

In 1841 a special prayer of thanks was offered up in Teffont Magna church for the queen's safe delivery of a princess. It seems unrealistic to expect a congregation of farming families, among whom the birth of a child was a regular but not always welcome event, to express gratitude to God for the queen's successful confinement. The fact that they did so is a reflection of the spirit of patriotism which the Napoleonic war had engendered.

Another effect of the war which was still being felt in Teffont Magna was the programme of land enclosure. This culminated in the Award of 1837, when the Earl of Pembroke reclaimed and enclosed much of his land in Teffont, including common land. John Lush's descendants and William Macey were deprived of their copy-holdings (although no doubt they were compensated). The remaining smallholders were in most cases allowed to retain a plot of land; but with no access to common land on which to graze their sheep, it was not easy for them to make a living.

The Maceys quickly turned their hands to other trades. The 1841 census identified a cooper, a draper, a tailor and a grocer, all with the name of Macey. William Chubb, who also lost land, was making good as a malster. The Malthouse was highly popular with the villagers, who brought their jugs to be filled with Chubb's ale at a hatch in one of its windows, which earned it the name 'The Hole in the Wall'. The village now had a blacksmith, a carpenter, a shoe maker, and even a baker (even though every housewife was expected to make her own bread).

The first impression one gains from the 1841 census is of a village which has adapted itself well to new conditions, given the variety of industries. On closer examination, however, the stark fact emerges that there were only two farmers left—Walter Fitz and Richard Norris—and that more than half the breadwinners were employed as farm labourers or domestic servants. The standard of living may have been higher than it was a hundred years earlier. (Certainly no paupers appear on the census). But it compares

sadly with the situation before enclosure, when each member of the community contributed to the age-old sheep-and-corn culture and shared its fruits.

The position of the shepherd had greatly deteriorated. His services were still in demand, but while hitherto the whole village had depended upon him, he now had little more value than other agricultural workers.

Farm wages in 1841 were poor. After the Swing riots they had risen temporarily, but mechanization had resulted in a pool of superfluous labour. Men capable of working the new machinery could demand a living wage, but the unskilled farm worker was lucky if he could get more than 7s per week. His lot was made especially hard by the steadily rising price of corn; this was caused on the one hand by the increased demand from an expanding urban population, and on the other by the Corn Laws, which prohibited the import of grain.

Until 1841 the names of farm workers were rarely recorded, unless they were accused of some misdemeanour. They were just a mass of faceless peasants who did not even get a gravestone when they died. But the census gave them each an identity, and offers us at least a narrow glimpse into their lives.

Take Job Kellow, a fairly typical farm labourer, forty years old, with a wife and seven children. How, one wonders, did he feed them on 7s per week? No doubt he had a bit of land attached to his rude cottage—enough to grow a few potatoes and keep a cow and a pig. At harvest time his wife and the older children would glean in the corn-fields, and collect anything edible or saleable in the forest. Hazel nuts were much sought after, for they could be ground up and used to replace some of the corn when making bread; sloes were also well worth picking, for they could be sold to pharmacies for the preparation of purgatives. No doubt there would have been many days when they went to bed cold and hungry. Perhaps they shivered a little less as a result of John Lush's legacy to provide blankets for the poor of the village.

Probably the best means available to the farm labourer of supplementing his wages was by poaching—not for his own table, but for the London gentry. Pheasant and partridge had become fashionable fare in London restaurants, but the chefs preferred birds without lead shot. As a consequence, provided he were able to avoid gamekeepers and man-traps, the poacher could make a nice profit from his snares. The stagecoaches had become notorious as conveyances of poached game. So all our Teffont Magna poacher had to do was to wait round the back of the Black Horse until the daily stagecoach drew in, and then, while Mistress Shergold attended to the passengers in the bar, hand over his booty to the driver.

According to the census, there were just nine people in the village of Teffont Magna employed as domestic servants, but there were probably many more working in houses outside. Most labouring families sent their daughters off into service before they were twelve, often to the towns, where country girls, who were reputed to be hardy and honest, were greatly sought after to work as servants.

Although Victorian employers were on the whole not noted for their generosity and kindliness, there were certain exceptions. One of these was Sydney Herbert.

George Herbert, 11th Earl of Pembroke (and landlord of Teffont Magna) had died in 1827 and had been succeeded by his son, Robert, who while still very young, eloped with an elderly Sicilian widow. Later, when he realized his mistake, he ran away to Paris to lead a life of debauchery, leaving the management of his estate in the hands of his step-brother, Sydney Herbert, an important public figure. He had become the Liberal M.P. for Wiltshire in 1835 (despite J T Mayne's efforts to 'excite the mob' against him), and subsequently held several senior Government appointments. He is perhaps best known for his sponsorship of Florence Nightingale.

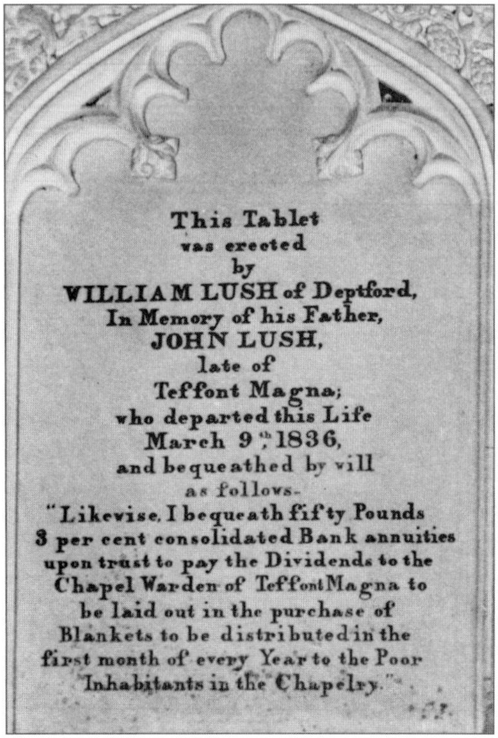

Memorial to John Lush.

Between his periods of office Sydney Herbert resided at Wilton, devoting himself to the administration of his brother's property. He became renowned for his exemplary treatment of his large workforce. He paid them fair wages and housed them well. His farm cottages, which included the four Hillside Cottages in Teffont Magna, won awards for their excellence. He even provided for his workers after retirement—an example of magnanimity almost unheard of at that time.

The 1841 census provides clear evidence that Teffont Evias village revolved around the manor. Out of a total of 44 people in employment, 18 were agricultural workers and 17 were servants. However, although John Mayne had absorbed much of the farming land in Teffont Evias, there were still four other farms left. William Cox ran the biggest one, Lower Farm, and Robert Fulcher had taken over The Mill. Although Richard Davies only had a few acres, he had established a cheese factory. There were two farm students in Teffont Evias at this time. One of them was Elias Squarey, who went on to become one of the greatest agricultural experts in the county.

John T Mayne bequeathed his estate to Emily, his eldest daughter, although the control of it was to remain in the hands of executors until 1852, when she reached the age of thirty. Even then, under the terms of the will, she was supposed to find a husband willing to pay off the £10,000 mortgage and change his name to Mayne. In 1852, however, she does not appear to have had a husband of any kind in view, but she gained possession of it just the same.

We know little of Emily's early life, beyond the fact that she was sent to school in France at the age of nine. When she returned two years later, Mrs Lear observed that she was 'not particularly improved by her French education'. One cannot help wondering in what way Mrs Lear found young Emily wanting. Was she perhaps too wilful? Certainly when she grew up she showed a will of her own. Emily had many fine qualities, but gentleness and amiability do not appear to have featured among them. Her relatives described her as 'hard as flint'.

She was certainly a hard-headed businesswoman. Although her uncle John Start took over the farm, Emily managed the estate, and made a tidy profit out of it. This was chiefly from rents, but she also made money from her woodland by selling timber and also bark (for the tanning industry.) It was perhaps as well for her sisters that John Mayne had left The Cottage for their use, with a right to free firewood; otherwise Emily might well have charged them for faggots—as she did her tenants—at the rate of five a shilling. A further source of income was provided by the sale of building material and paving stones from the quarry (a trade revived by the opening of the Salisbury-Yeovil railway line), and she established a kiln to convert rubble into lime, for which there was a demand by farmers in acid soil areas.

Some of her profits went back into the estate. She planted a considerable number of trees, and acquired earth from a railway cutting to dam the stream and convert a muddy pond into a fair-sized ornamental lake.

Emily possessed one accomplishment generally approved of in Victorian ladies: watercolour painting. She also engaged in glass staining, and created a window for the Ley chapel in memory of her father. But it was too crude for the taste of a later generation, so it was taken out and binned.

The rector of Teffont Evias was still Mr Samuel Broomshead Ward. He was a successful and popular minister, and the church attracted large congregations. There had been a religious revival throughout the country at the end of the 18th century initiated by the Godless behaviour of the French revolutionaries, but Teffont Evias church boasted an exceptionally high attendance, considering the size of the parish. Sunday morning congregations averaged 80, and rose to 150 in the afternoon, when Mr Ward gave his weekly sermon, attracting visitors from other parishes.

Perhaps they sang Cecil Frances Alexander's new hymn 'All things bright and beautiful', accompanied on a fine 18th-century 'cello. On the installation of the organ in the 1860s the anonymous fiddler sold his cello to Frank Scammell, the verger, who subsequently gave it to Salisbury Museum. The hymn is occasionally sung in Teffont Evias church today—with the omission of the politically incorrect verse:

'The rich man in his castle, the poor man at his gate
God made them high and lowly and ordered their estate'.

The 'lowly' among the mid 19th-century congregation, however, would not have disputed the claim—any more than they would have questioned that their place in the church was on the cold, hard benches at the very back of the nave.

The rich men of Wiltshire were to be found on farms rather than in castles, and they were getting richer. The rural economy was booming. The growing urban population still consumed all the corn the country could grow. Even the repeal of the Corn Laws in 1846, which cleared the way for the free import of corn, rang no alarm bells. Indeed, until the mid 1870s the amounts of imported grain were neither large enough nor cheap enough to cause any problems. The large farms were putting as much land as possible under the plough. In a letter dated 1845 Miss Wyndham observed: 'nearly all Teffont Down has been given over to wheat and turnips'. (Turnips were used as winter fodder for the all-important sheep.) The poet Matthew Arnold bemoaned the fact that there were no places left for wild flowers to grow.

Even the farm workers seemed to be having less difficulty in making ends meet. By 1851 their wages had risen to the unprecedented sum of 10s per week, and the number of agricultural labourers in Teffont Magna had risen to 50 (including 5 shepherds). 24 men were employed by Edward Harris, who had acquired Norris's farm and doubled its acreage. A further 8 were employed by John, the son of Mary Ann Shergold, the innkeeper. Job Kellow was still employed as a labourer. Most of his children appear to have survived; two of his sons were now shepherds, and the two youngest children were in school.

The notion of providing affordable schooling for the children of the poor was introduced by the Victorian liberals. Emily Mayne set up a school for the children of her tenants in a cottage in the manor grounds. (The Old School House, converted into a cottage, is still there today.) It made a good impression on an Education Enquiry inspector in 1858. He recorded that there were 30-40 children, and that the mistress was 'a person of fair address'. Whether this compliment refers to Ely Goodfellow, recorded as 'school mistress' in the 1851 census, or to Emily herself is not clear. Job Kellow's children would not have qualified to attend Emily Mayne's school. They would either have gone to a school in Teffont Magna run by a widow named Jane Crowther, whom the inspector described as 'a dame of limited acquirements', or to the church school in Dinton, where 50-60 children were taught by 'a mistress with a master (a one-legged man)'.

The village industries in Teffont Magna were obviously flourishing. It might not have been the peaceful place people often imagine. In addition to the noise of the blacksmiths striking their anvils and the coopers knocking their barrels into shape, there would have been the din from the carpenter's shop, where Henry Ford employed 8 men. They left no clues as to what they produced. There was certainly no shortage of local material: hazel for tool-handles and scaffolding, and oak or elm for carts and household furniture. They were perhaps involved in repairs to the church, which amounted to £42 in 1847. There is no doubt about one thing they would have produced: the sound of a great deal of hammering and sawing.

Teffont Evias would have been a quieter place. The majority of the villagers still worked as farm labourers or as domestic servants of the manor. While Teffont Magna had 28 people involved in village industries, Evias had only 5. They also recorded 5 paupers in 1851: four old women, including 2 retired servants from the manor, and one old man. There was a village Friendly Society, established in 1830, through which, if a man paid 2s 6d every eight weeks, he could expect financial support when he was down on his luck. Women, however, and old men—i.e. those over the age of 45—were not eligible for membership. The workhouse in Tisbury was all they could look forward to.

There was no longer a baker in Teffont Magna, but there was a shopkeeper, an eating-house keeper —and a game keeper. Perhaps too many pheasant had been finding there way up to London on the stagecoach. But the system was breaking up. The railways were gradually taking the traffic off the roads. As Emily Mayne's lake filled up with water, an increasing number of trains were chugging their way into London. The days of travel by stagecoach were numbered.

Nevertheless, the horse and cart remained the main means of travel for the villagers. For those who did not possess a vehicle of their own, there was the village carrier. Both the Teffonts possessed at least one full-time or part-time carrier, who would be employed to carry a range of cargoes, from peat for the hearth to pigs for the market.

In 1859, when Emily Mayne was 37, her life changed dramatically: she married William Fane de Salis. Ten years her senior, de Salis was the descendant of a noble Swiss family and a highly successful businessman (he eventually became the chairman of the P & O shipping company). He seems to have been the sort of man who would appreciate a woman with a few brains in her head. The bishop came from Salisbury to conduct the marriage ceremony in Teffont Evias church. Not surprisingly, de Salis did not take his wife's name; neither, it seems, did he pay off the mortgage.

Emily left Teffont and went to live in her husband's house, Dawley Court, in Middlesex. One gains the

Pembroke Farm cottages, which won awards for their excellence.

impression that she closed her account book, locked the door, threw her hat in the air and went off to enjoy the high life. Her departure must have been a severe blow for the residents of Teffont Evias. Sarah Mayne and her remaining unmarried daughter left at the same time and went to live in Clifton (Bristol). The manor appears to have been completely closed up. At all events, none of the servants, indoor or outdoor, remained.

Home Farm House, with the shop run by Ethelinda Bugg.

John Coles was left to run Teffont Evias manor farm, but he employed only half as many men as Start had done in 1851. Some time in the 1860s Edward Drew took over the farm, and for the first time in village records, employed women as well as men as workers. They expected to work shorter hours, but were cheaper than men to employ. Nevertheless, the number of men in the village employed as farm labourers was considerably higher than ten years earlier. Thomas Bugg now ran Home Farm with a shop managed by his wife, Ethelinda, in the farmhouse. (The house is still called Home Farm House, but both the shop and the farm have gone). Henry Goodfellow, the last generation of that name to own the mill, had left in 1835, and it had been taken over by Thomas Bugg's brother John. On his death, his widow Elizabeth became the miller, and continued to grind until her death in 1885. Other members of the community found alternative ways of earning their crust: in the smithy, the carpenter's shop, the stone quarry and the lime kilns. The village had also acquired a post-mistress. This may have been due to a post office official named Anthony Trollope, who had toured the area a few years earlier and been appalled by the chaotic arrangements he found for the delivery of mail.

In Teffont Magna, Edward Harris had increased the size of his farm to 1051 acres and was now employing 30 men and 19 boys. Sad to say, Henry Ford had died, and his carpentry business with him. There were two other men plying his trade, and his widow, Mary, was running a shop. Other businesses in the village included the Macey family of coopers, a partnership of plumbers/glaziers, a saddler and harness-maker, a grocer, a blacksmith, a laundress and a choice of shoe makers. There was even a resident fund-holder. Where services were concerned, Teffont Magna in the 1860s and 1870s would have been hard to beat.

The Reverend Samuel Broomshead Ward, the long-standing rector of Teffont Evias, died in 1866. His memorial is a very modest one, tucked away behind the church. In life, he was by contrast very conspicuous, whether strutting around his garden wearing yellow gloves, or delivering eloquent sermons from his pulpit. He was neither shy of inviting the Wyndhams to tea nor of giving his patron, John Mayne, a piece of his mind. The Wyndhams were inclined to sneer at him for his manner of gardening, but the garden he left (in the grounds of the old rectory, now named Bridges) is the most beautiful in Teffont Evias.

In 1870, as a result of the Education Act, a recognized Elementary School was opened in Dinton, which was considered within easy walking distance for children from Teffont. In the first year, seven Teffont children were admitted, and in the following year ten, their ages ranging from 7 to 10 years; almost all were the sons of agricultural labourers. The school summer holidays were programmed to coincide with harvest-time, since it was recognized that no child would be allowed the luxury of sitting at a desk once the important business of haymaking and harvesting had begun.

Six years later Teffont Magna acquired its own Elementary School for the children of both Magna and Evias. It had been built at a cost of £500, raised by public subscription. This suggests both prosperity and optimism on the part of the villagers.

They were no doubt unaware of the significance of an event which occurred in 1875: the first shipment of grain arriving from the North American prairies.

The grain proved to be of high quality, its price was low, and there was an almost unlimited supply of it available. The Tory landowners were not slow to grasp its significance. They demanded the re-imposition of tariff barriers, but the government would not listen. As they saw it, the wealth of the country was in industry, and if their overseas customers were willing to pay for manufactured goods in the form of cheap food for the factory workers, so much the better. To make matters worse for the local farmers, refrigerated mutton and lamb began to arrive from New Zealand.

The Wiltshire farmers might have had a better chance of surviving the crisis had it not been for three consecutive years of bad harvests from 1878 to 1880. 1879 was especially disastrous: continuous rain not only ruined the crops, but also resulted in disease ('the bane') among the sheep, which was so severe that it wiped out entire flocks. The disaster might have been in part avoided if the farmers had not some years earlier replaced their hardy, thin-fleeced Wiltshire Horn sheep by Hampshire Down; this variety produced better wool, but was much more vulnerable to disease.

Three little maids from school—Teffont Magna Elementary School, opened 1917.

The corn-and-sheep agriculture, for so long the mainstay of the Wiltshire farmer, never recovered. The price of wheat gradually slipped back from 58s 3d per quarter in 1873 to 26s 2d in 1896, and the price of

Early school days.

lamb and wool suffered a similar decline. As a consequence there was a gradual slide back into poverty for much of the farming community, and not a few bankruptcies within the region.

It appears that in the Teffonts there was less severe hardship than in many other village communities. They were perhaps fortunate in belonging to manors whose proprietors had other sources of income. The Earl of Pembroke's lucrative estates in Ireland allowed him to reduce his rents, enabling his tenants to survive. Married as she was to a wealthy husband, Emily de Salis could also afford to reduce her rents.

The dilemma faced by both landlord and tenant are demonstrated by the experiences of John Keevil, who had taken over the lease of the 1000-acre Pembroke-owned Manor Farm in Teffont Magna in the 1870s at a rent of £900 per annum. By 1891 it had been reduced to £425, but Keevil remained in arrears until it was further reduced to £333 the following year. Keevil was the only large-scale farmer left in Teffont Magna. Walter Fitz had died some time in the 1840s, and his farm was taken over by William Wyndham.

Since the community of Teffont Magna remained dependent on agriculture, it is remarkable that it survived as well as it did. The 1881 census shows no reduction in the number of resident agricultural workers; neither is there a significant decline in tradesmen. There was no longer a shoe maker, but there was now a milliner. Chubb was still running the Hole in the Wall, and the Black Horse was still open. The number of children attending school had increased, but this was probably owing to a ridiculous new law (or so it was held to be!) that required boys to remain at school until the age of eleven. The

Emily de Salis. *Courtesy of W Keatinge.* (VK)

William Fane de Salis, husband of Emily. *Courtesy of W Keatinge.* (VK)

decline in the village economy, however, is clearly indicated by the fact that the population decreased from 288 to 192 between 1880 and 1904, while,during the same period, the rateable value slumped from £1883 to £960.

The economy of Teffont Evias appears to have held up rather better. There was no significant decrease in population or rateable value. The pattern of the community shows little change. Most of the land was still in the hands of just two farmers: Sydney Harnett, who ran Manor Farm, and Thomas Bugg, who had also become an insurance agent. The amount of arable land had been severely cut down, however. Barley was the main crop, with hay cut from the pastures.

One gains the impression that Emily de Salis, who had worked so hard to make money out of her estate before her marriage, no longer gave a fig as to whether it made a profit or not. The scrapbook she kept from 1878 until the mid 1890s contains nothing relating to agriculture or the economy. It chiefly contains newspaper reports of the doings of the great and the good, together with mementoes of her travels.

But Emily was not completely cut off from Teffont Evias. She and her husband took regular holidays in the manor. She took the opportunity of her visits to do some good works. In 1884 she built a pair of alms-houses, which were designated to remain as such for 100 years: two solid dwellings each designed to hold two people. (They were later sold and joined together to form a private house now called Acacia Cottage). She is also accredited with laying on piped water throughout the village in 1893. The project—to supply pure water to both villages by putting a pipeline from the springhead at Teffont Magna—was in fact initiated in Teffont Magna. Perhaps Emily paid for the installation of the pipe and stand-pipes at her end of the line.

Although the stream flowing from the springhead was easily accessible to the inhabitants of both villages, by the time it reached Teffont Evias it would have been polluted in a variety of ways. The villagers had been obliged to draw well-water for drinking. Although drawing water at a well has a romantic ring to it, hauling up heavy buckets from many feet below ground and then trudging home with them was a chore, which the villagers were no doubt grateful to be spared.

Emily and her husband showed great interest in Teffont Evias church. They re-roofed part of it, added a vestry, and tiled the floor of the Ley chapel with tiles decorated with the de Salis coronet and the Mayne crest (which can be seen today). Kitty Keatinge had misgivings about this, suspecting that the tiles hid a more interesting flagstone floor, perhaps incorporating old Hungerford gravestones.

Emily's greatest contribution to the church arises from her acquaintance with her husband's distant relative, Baron Henri de Triqueti, a successful sculptor. Amongst other achievements, he had executed the bronze door for La Madeleine in Paris. He was, however, experimenting with a new technique—a refined type of mosaic known as tarsia. His inspiration apparently came from the pictorial marble mosaic pavements on the floors of Sienna Cathedral. His chief innovation was to apply the technique to a wall-hanging instead of a floor-covering. His works did not have immediate appeal. In fact, Emily was only his second customer after he had been working in the medium for ten years. The first was the South Kensington Museum.

His tarsia picture entitled 'The Choir of Angels' was installed on the wall of the Ley chapel, Teffont Evias in October 1863. It is composed of softly-toned marbles of white, blue and grey, with definition provided by lines of black and red cement. The surface is so smooth that for many years it was thought to be an oil painting.

Emily de Salis subsequently recommended de Triqueti's work to Queen Victoria. Her letter may have tipped the balance in favour of commissioning the Baron to design panels for the walls of the Albert Memorial Chapel, Windsor Castle; the Queen favoured this plan, but her architect, George Gilbert Scott, had argued it was impractical. The only other de Triqueti tarsia in this country is in University College, London. 'The Choir of Angels' is thus a rare example of de Triqueti's extraordinary form of art, rendered especially interesting by the fact that it hangs in the modest setting of a little country church.

'The Choir of Angels', a tarsia by Henri de Triqueti.

CHAPTER TWELVE

WAR AND PEACE

Margaret Mayne, whose epitaph records that she was 'the last of the Maynes to own the Manor of Teffont Evias', inherited the property on the death of her sister Emily de Salis in 1896. Her father, John T Mayne, would have been proud to see the manor once again held by someone bearing his name—but appalled by his daughter's behaviour. Unwilling to leave her home in Clifton, Bristol, in 1897 she leased the manor house to Charles Maudslay, a wealthy engineer, and entrusted the management of the estate to a lawyer named Merley, who proved to be as much of a rascal as the one who had cheated her grandfather. He ended up in Salisbury gaol, but not before he had lined his pockets at Margaret's expense.

It is apparent from the photograph of the cottage rented by Mr Sutton that Merley did not waste much money on the upkeep of the estate cottages; there is no glass in the windows, and the thatch is in an appalling state of repair. However, Mr Sutton and his wife appear fairly philosophical about the state of their home, which they had begun to rent in 1851 for 1s 6d per week. Some fifty draughty years later, when the photograph was taken, Mr Sutton was ninety and his wife seventy-five. Both are obviously dressed in their Sunday best, Mrs Sutton wearing over her skirt a spotless white apron—an article of apparel in which all the village women took great pride.

Perhaps Margaret had begun to have misgivings about her lawyer's integrity by 1904, since, when the old mill burnt down that year, she entrusted the task of disposing of the ruins to her nephew, Gerald, even though he was in India. He sent instructions to a local builder to use the stones to construct a house at the top of the hill above the mill-stream at a cost of no more than £500. The result was the house called Goldens, which still stands in this delightful setting.

Having had part of her inheritance stolen from her while she lived, Margaret gave away another large part of it on her death to a clergyman who had prayed with her during the last lonely years in Clifton before her death in 1905.

Margaret's sister Ellen inherited the manor; as a result of having married an Irish barrister named Maurice Keatinge, she was the first of the Keatinges (the present landlords) to own the manor. She and her family had spent a lot of time in Teffont Evias and had a great fondness for it, but she was now an eighty-year-old widow, and preferred to spend her remaining days near her children in Oxford. On her death in 1907 the manor was inherited by her eldest son, Richard. He was a doctor who for financial reasons had been forced to live abroad. A country estate without the means to maintain it was therefore of little interest to him, so he put it up for sale. His younger brothers Gerald and Walter managed to raise the money to buy it from him, and although he was still serving with the ICS in India, Gerald became the new lord of the manor.

Even though the villagers rarely caught a glimpse of their lord or lady of the manor after Emily de Salis's death, they had a substitute to whom they could doff their caps in the persons of Mr Charles Maudslay and his sister. They lived in great style, employed a large staff of servants and by all accounts expected to be treated with the respect due to lords of the manor, if not princes of the royal blood. Maudslay would have dearly liked to own the manor, and on Margaret's death he offered to buy it for £20,000 (to include the family portraits!). Generous though the offer sounded, it was not accepted.

Although Maudslay's £200 per year rent gave him tenancy of the manor house and 23 acres of grounds, it did not include the woodlands. As well as deciduous forest, these comprised a large plantation of firs, including 100,000 larches planted in 1904, a valuable source of income for the Keatinges. Maudslay did, however, enjoy shooting rights throughout the entire estate, and he made frequent complaints about the felling of the trees, which, he maintained, interfered with his sport. But Gerald Keatinge ignored them, for he needed the money. He had netted a useful £400 shortly after he and his brother had bought the manor in 1908, and the timber continued to yield about £100 per year. He invested a proportion of this in replanting, enabling Thomas Mullins, the woodman, to earn up to £40 in a year.

Charles Maudslay had brought along with him his groom, a young fellow called Robert Lee (his daughter, Alice Lee, now aged 92, still lives in Teffont). When a few years later Maudslay replaced his pony and trap by a car, Robert exchanged his bowler hat for a chauffeur's cap. The vehicle was, of course, a Maudslay, for Charles's firm was one of the pioneers in the motor industry. It may well have been the first car to be seen in the Nadder Valley.

The Maudslays were not popular in the village, and they were reputed to be

Mr and Mrs Sutton at Goldens Cottage in the late 19th century.

The Teffont Evias General Store in 1905.

harsh employers. Nevertheless, the majority of the villagers were dependent on the manor and its tenants for their livelihood. The manor employed not only the domestic servants and estate workers, but also indirectly the village tradesmen and artisans: the blacksmith, the miller, the carpenters, the carters, the shop-keepers and the newly installed dressmaker. Moreover, whether the villagers liked them or not, the fact that such high-class gentry chose to live in their village's splendid manor house enabled the inhabitants to hold their heads a little higher and to look down their noses at their neighbours up the road in Teffont Magna.

It is evident from the 1901 census that Teffont Magna was no longer the prosperous village it had been before the agricultural depression of the late 19th century. The number of its inhabitants has shrunk, and most are classified as labourers of one sort or another. Many of the old familiar names have disappeared, although there are still several Larkhams and Kellows around. Job Kellow's son, Thomas, was running the village shop, together with his wife, Elizabeth. There was still a blacksmith and a saddler in the village, and George Jukes, previously a general dealer, now styled himself 'game dealer'. He would have had access to game from the large farm his family owned in Dinton and probably from Maudslay's bag as well. No doubt the best specimens were destined for the fleshpots of London, but there were probably rabbits and pigeons for local consumption. He was apparently a fishmonger as well. Bessie Dyer, who lived nearby, would probably have been recognizable by her red hands—for she was the village laundress.

There were only 37 agricultural workers living in Teffont Magna in 1901 (down from 67 in 1891). Some of the labourers, no doubt, worked for Daniel Coombes, who in 1903 had taken over Keevil's lease at Manor Farm; others were very likely employed by Wyndham or on the more distant Pembroke estates. However far away it was, they would have had to walk to their place of work, unless they could afford one of the heavy, solid-tyred bicycles which had recently come on to the market. They could not even look forward to getting a jug of ale at the end of their long day's work, for there was no maltster in the village, and the Hole in the Wall had (at least temporarily) closed its shutters. To be sure, the Black Horse was still functioning, but with beer at 2d a pint, a visit to its taproom was more a social activity than a means of slaking the thirst.

The low price of corn, which was crippling the farmers, meant that the labourer's wages went further, but he was still only just above the poverty line. He would very likely have had an allotment, where he would have grown potatoes and other vegetables to help feed his family. Nevertheless, it is unlikely that his wife had much of her meagre housekeeping money left over to spend in the Kellows' shop. She may have bought the odd luxury such as a packet of tea for herself, an ounce of tobacco for her husband and a halfpenny-worth of 'hard-bake' toffee for the children, but most of her pennies will have been spent on essentials such as sewing cotton, Sunlight soap, candles and paraffin for the lamps now in regular use. (The towns were able to enjoy lighting and cooking by gas, but the gas-pipes did not—and never would—extend into the Nadder valley). If she was in luck, the labourer's wife might have found Elizabeth Kellow behind the counter. According to her great-granddaughter, Barbara Baker, Elizabeth was a big liability to the business, for she was too soft-hearted to charge the poor for their purchases.

Charles Maudslay and his sister.

The relative prosperity of Teffont Evias is demonstrated by the photograph dated 1905 of one of its two village shops, with a well-stocked window and notices outside advertising drapery, groceries and boots and shoes. Some of the shops' customers must have come from surrounding villages, for there was not a big working population left in Teffont Evias (only 7 agricultural labourers in 1901). The staff of Teffont Manor may well have patronized the shop for the material for their dresses, but they would have had to go further afield for the corsets, which they are so obviously wearing in their photograph. They may well have got them by mail order from the Landport Drapery Bazaar (for 2s 11d, including postage), as advertised in the Salisbury Journal.

The Maudslays' staff (Robert Lee stands on the extreme right).

Charles Maudslay with two of his cars: A pram-hood model (to accommodate wearers of silk hats) of c1913, and partly in view, a tourer, 40-horse-power, of 1909.

It was a good year for the Teffont Evias quarries. They had been leased by T T Gething & Co, and they were commissioned to provide stone for the repaving of Westminster Abbey. The lime kilns in Carter's Lane were doing good business. To facilitate transport of unusable stone from Butts Hill quarry, a linking tramway had been built, along which ran trucks drawn by donkeys to the lime kilns in Carters Lane.

One luxury which both the villages enjoyed in equal measure was presented to them in 1908: the old-age pension. Known as 'the Lloyd George', it amounted to five shillings per week for those fortunate enough to reach the age of seventy. Not a fortune—but enough to keep them out of the dreaded workhouse.

The traditional corn-and-sheep farming was still being carried on to a small extent. There were still flocks of sheep to be seen grazing the downs, and three shepherds and a hurdle-maker are recorded in the census covering Teffont Magna. The Teffont Evias estate still ran a flock of 400 sheep at least until 1906. However, since most of the agrarian land in Evias had been converted to pasture, it is possible that they were grass sheep rather than hurdle sheep, raised for their wool more than for their use as fertilizers. The farmers had apparently overcome their prejudice against 'teat-pulling', as they had contemptuously described the industry of their Northern Wiltshire neighbours, for dairy cattle had been introduced on the estate. The recording of a head dairyman in addition to a stockman on the 1901 census suggests quite a big herd.

Horses were still the main source of power on Teffont's farms in the early 20th century.

There were other attempts made at diversification. As many as 27 orchards are recorded in the two Teffont villages, and they produced interesting varieties of apples, including Copper Crowns, Russets and Lady Henicar, but they were perhaps not grown in sufficient quantities to be commercially viable. However, the Teffont Evias postmaster's brother took some cuttings of Yeate's Pippin with him when he emigrated to Australia, and made a commercial success out of growing them. Tobacco was also cultivated in Teffont Magna for a few years from 1910 for a Salisbury company, H Stevens & Co.

The celebration of the coronation of George V at Teffont Manor in 1911.

There was still very little mechanization on the farms. The 1901 Teffont Magna census records two 'farm engine drivers'; they were most likely driving the threshing engines, which had caused riots when first introduced in the 19th century, but which were now accepted and in fairly common use. Alternatively, they might have driven the steam tractors which the Earl of Pembroke had introduced on his estate.

But the horse was still the main source of power on the farms, providing enough work to keep blacksmiths in business in both our villages. One of Paffard Keatinge-Clay's boyhood memories is watching with wonder as Harry Bull, the Teffont Evias blacksmith, shod a shire horse, fashioning the new shoe by hammering it out on his anvil. The farm carter had become an increasingly important employee. He was in charge of all the horses on a farm. To him belonged most of the horse-brassses seen today on the walls of village inns. The horses may have belonged to the farmer, but the brasses were his, and he took them with him if he changed his employer.

One of Alice Lee's earliest memories of Teffont is the celebration party held at the manor in 1911 to mark the coronation of King George V. The Maudslays obviously scored points with the village on this occasion: the gardens were illuminated with lanterns, there was feasting and dancing and the band of the 4th Wiltshire Regiment played throughout the evening.

A few months before the beginning of the First World War, Teffont Evias became the scene of an extraordinary drama. The scene was in fact set the previous year, following the death of the rector, the Rev John Hewitt. Gerald Keatinge and his wife, Polly, home on leave from India, took the opportunity to appoint a new rector. The living of £123 per annum with its grand rectory attracted several applicants. From among them the Keatinges selected the Rev Sir Douglas Scott, Bart. His induction took place before a large congregation in June 1913.

The Rev Scott moved into the rectory, undertook some expensive improvements and furnished it with Maples' best furniture at a cost of £400. He received it all on credit, of course—as a gentleman customarily did. Unfortunately, however, he was already deeply in debt. On 14 February 1914 he was declared bankrupt (the case was reported at length in the Salisbury Journal), and on the 28th his furniture was auctioned by the Official Receiver. Members of his congregation may have hung their heads, but those attending the sale declared it to be 'the best in the neighbourhood for many years'.

But this was only the first act of the drama. Shortly afterwards the Rev Sir Douglas Scott was arrested for bigamy and subsequently defrocked. Moreover, he had committed one further offence which the gentlemen of the district may have found even more shocking: he had falsely claimed to hold HM commissions in both the armed services.

As early as March 1913 a Wiltshire Tory MP, Charles Bathurst (who was later to become closely associated with Teffont Magna), drew the Government's attention to the fact that the country was dependent on imports for four-fifths of its food. But his protest was rather huffily dismissed. Did we not have the most powerful navy in the world, perfectly able to protect our shipping routes should the necessity arise? When war broke out in August 1914 the Government did little to change the situation.

Nevertheless, the early years of the war were beneficial for Wiltshire agriculture. The large body of soldiers in training camps on Salisbury Plain gave a boost to the local farming industry, since they required not only food for men and horses but also straw for mattresses. The Army paid well, if not always promptly, for their supplies, and the farmers were able to take advantage of a large supply of valuable horse-manure.

In 1916 the Germans started to attack the grain-ships from America with U-boats, a menace which the Navy were unable to overcome. Consequently there was an urgent need for more home-grown cereals. Although most skilled farm workers, above a certain age, were given exemption from recruitment, the farmers experienced an ever-increasing shortage of labour, while the Government pressed them to grow more crops. Demands were made that more land should be brought under cultivation, causing some resentment among the farmers, since they had just turned it over to pasture. The Teffont Evias pastures were now supporting 200 head of cattle. Moreover, more cultivation required more labour. It was a vicious circle.

The government-appointed Agricultural Executive Committee introduced various measures to solve the problem. Children were allowed to leave school at twelve (rather than the legal age of thirteen) so that the boys could work in the fields and their sisters take over the housekeeping, allowing their mothers to join the labour force. This must have come as a relief to the Teffont school teacher, Mrs Delia Palmer, who taught unaided an average of 55 pupils ranging from five to thirteen years old. Beyond the age of eleven or so, few of the boys were interested in 'book-learning'.

Mechanization became the order of the day, and steam ploughs were offered to the farmers, who found them too cumbersome to be much use. Motor tractors were a better proposition, and a few of these were made available; one was parked at Dinton Station in 1917 for the use of the local farmers. Soldiers were also turned over to agricultural labour, but they were not very popular with the farmers. They did not come cheaply—4s a day—and most of them couldn't tell a weasel from a mangel-wurzel. It was suspected that they only came into agriculture to avoid being sent to the front. And who could blame them?

Where war casualties were concerned, our two villages escaped comparatively lightly, only losing six of their sons. One of them, Lieutenant Nigel Trotter, was Gerald Keatinge's nephew, whose parents,

Alexander Trotter.

Alys Trotter.

Alexander and Alys Trotter, came to live in Teffont. The other five young men who lost their lives were Lance-Corporal Percy Smith (killed during the first battle of the war in November 1914), Private Francis Kellow, Private James Mould, Private W H Randall and Trooper Elliott. Ralph Larkin died of pneumonia, but his widow, Lilian, lived on for many years and became an indispensable member of village society: she took charge of arrivals and departures, being midwife and (as was customary) layer-out of the dead.

A building named the Teffont Reading Room was erected in memory of the war dead. In fact it was used for playing rather than reading: billiards, darts and card games, and dances were sometimes held there. It is still in existence, but since we now have a well-appointed village hall, it is rented out to a small industry.

The fate of their menfolk in Flanders was not the only thing the villagers had to worry about during the war. Although the national shortage of food did not hit the country dwellers as hard as the town folk, they were not immune from it. Flour especially was in short supply and adulterated. The villagers were fortunate to have the produce of their gardens, although they did not regard vegetables as serious food; rearing pigs—which provided almost the only meat many of them tasted—was made difficult by lack of feed. Fruit was widely grown, especially currants, berries and plums, which could be converted into money in the Salisbury market or made into jam for the winter. A ready source of manure was provided by the privy at the top of the garden.

A disaster which occurred in 1915 was an Act of God rather than a consequence of war. The Black Horse was struck by lightning; its thatch caught fire, and it was almost completely burnt down. It was perhaps fortunate for the villagers that the Methodist chapel had closed down in 1905 and that its premises—ironically—had been taken over by a brewer. But the fire had consumed the greatly prized banner of the Teffont Magna Friendly Society, which had been stored in the Black Horse.

The end of the war brought big changes in the agricultural scene. The Board of Agriculture had

The Black Horse Inn, burnt down in 1915.

hoped to encourage farmers to continue producing grain by offering guaranteed prices. But at the same time they established a minimum wage for labourers of 25s per week. Not excessive, by any standards. However, many landowners found they were left with too small a margin of profit, and a significant number sold off their land. These included the Earl of Pembroke, who in 1919 sold his estate at Teffont Magna.

The buyer was Charles Bathurst, now Lord Bledisloe. Although King George V once called him Lord Bloody Slow, he appears to have risen quite rapidly during the last six years. Not only had he been raised to the peerage, he had also held several important Government appointments.

The residents of Teffont Magna may have had a few misgivings about their new lord. To be sure, he had recognized the folly of the Government in allowing British agriculture to be ruined by the import of American grain; but, at the same time, he had opposed setting a minimum wage for agricultural workers and deplored the fact that they were given a bit of land with their cottages. However, he proved to be a good landlord: he repaired his tenants' cottages, put in concrete floors, and gave them each a Virginia creeper. (The latter proved a mixed blessing, since it spread over areas where it was not wanted.) In general, Lord Bledisloe was well liked.

One person who did not subscribe to this view was Edith Olivier. When, on the death of their father in 1920, she and her sister Mildred were looking for a house, Bledisloe agreed to rent them Fitz House. He had just finished repairing and renovating it, possibly with the intention of living there himself. But he settled for retaining one room—the Cheese Room—for his occasional visits to the village. Edith was delighted, for she had wanted to live in Fitz House ever since her childhood, when she had described it as 'a most romantic house in the prettiest of all Wiltshire villages'.

The romance, however, began to wear off and the visitor to the Cheese Room to acquire increasingly bad odour when rain came in through the roof and the hot-water system packed up. When in 1922 Lord Pembroke offered Edith The Daye House on the Wilton estate, he referred to Bledisloe as a bloodsucker and his agent Kennedy Shaw as a viper.

Nevertheless, the sisters enjoyed the two years they stayed in Teffont—especially when it wasn't raining. They lived quietly, but took an interest in the life of the village. It was not until after Mildred's death a few years later that Edith started writing and became the central figure in a coterie of budding artists and poets. Since she was already very interested in art, it is surprising that she never made any mention

Two ladies, believed to be Edith and Mildred Olivier, in Fitz House garden, c1920.

of the family of accomplished artists who were near neighbours in Teffont. They were Fanny, Lucy, Gideon and Harry Fidler. The two sisters remained amateurs, combining their talent with housekeeping and gardening, but their brothers became professional artists. Harry, who studied at the Herkomer School in Bushey, specialised in impressionistic painting of country life, while Gideon favoured domestic and genre subjects. Both the brothers exhibited widely, and Harry Fidler is now internationally renowned.

Despite its imperfections, Lord Bledisloe found a new tenant for Fitz House within a few months: Colonel Charles French. He was a passionate garden builder. I use the word advisedly, for he built rather than planted. With the help of a gardener/stone-mason he built paths, steps, terraces, a summer house, and walls large and small, which he lined with beech and yew hedges to produce 'garden rooms'. He gives the impression of a man so engrossed in his hobby that he would hardly have noticed water coming in from the roof or not coming out of the hot tap.

Gerald Keatinge returned home from India in 1921. One of his first acts was to give the Maudslays notice to quit. The Maudslays were dismayed; they could see no justification for his refusal to renew their lease. Either they were completely unaware of their unpopularity, or they considered the opinion of the labouring classes to be of no importance. But Gerald Keatinge was a fair man, and he respected the judgement of the villagers. So the Maudslays departed, seething with resentment, which was intensified by the fact that they had recently presented the church with a new organ.

The Keatinges continued to lease the manor while they lived in Goldens (the house built with the

Gerald Keatinge walking through his woodlands.

stones from the burnt-out mill); although less grand, it was considerably cosier. Gerald showed little interest in farming. He sold Ley Farm, and was possibly able to pay off the £10,000 mortgage on the estate as a result.

He leased the two remaining farms: the Mill and Home Farm. The latter was efficiently run for many years by Joseph Fennell. However, the fact that Mrs Fennell continued to use part of her farmhouse as a shop probably indicates that the farm was not making a big profit. Gerald Keatinge appears to have confined his interest to the woodland, which as he grew older he valued increasingly for its aesthetic rather than its commercial quality. He undertook a lot of planting, even setting up a nursery in which he grew oaks from acorns.

There were new tenants in the manor: Mr and Mrs Kenneth Walker. He was a highly respected retired naval commander and explorer. He did, however, have certain eccentricities: he decorated the rooms of the manor with souvenirs of his explorations, which included poisoned arrows, spears, clubs and other deadly weapons, all combined with small human bones. Despite this, the Walkers were well liked in the village. Fourteen-year-old Alice Lee had her first job with them as one of their three kitchen maids.

Gerald Keatinge became especially fond of another of his tenants, Henry Warwick Howard, who with his wife had taken a lease of The Cottage soon after Ellen Keatinge's death in 1907. Henry Howard was an accomplished artist, but, like so many of Teffont's residents, he had been bitten by the gardening bug; by the time Gerald came home he had virtually abandoned his canvasses, and was creating a picture made of living plants. He had become such an institution in the village that the Keatinges began to refer to The Cottage as 'Howard's House'.

It was a name which stuck. Even though Henry Howard died more than 70 years ago, and the house has been turned into a gracious country house hotel, it still keeps his homely name. Its opening date is usually given as 1989, but in actual fact it first opened its doors to guests in the 1930s. It was then that the widowed Mrs Howard decided to supplement her income by taking in paying guests. Although the guests would have enjoyed a garden at least as attractive as the one there today, the amenities of the house and the regime under which they lived would have been very different. The plumbing would have been rudimentary, and the rules of the house, imposed by the formidable Mrs Howard, stern and inflexible.

Teffont Magna's inn, the Black Horse, had been rebuilt, but its proprietors, William and Lavinia

Farmer, devoted much of their time to farming. Theirs was the smallest of the three remaining farms in Teffont Magna. Lord Bledisloe had bought back Fitz Farm, which had for many years been a part of the Wyndham estate. It continued to be farmed by a Dinton man, Jesse Ash, until it was bought in 1939 by Charles Giles.

At the time Bledisloe acquired Teffont Magna, Dan Coombes was the tenant of Manor Farm. It had become a mixed farm, with sheep, cattle, pigs, chickens and wheat, struggling to make a profit. The photograph shows a farm worker, Frank Hardiman, demonstrating a contraption for sowing seed: a wide drill is precariously mounted on a wheel-barrow, looking as it might have been invented by Heath Robinson himself. But Lady Bledisloe and her husband's agent, the formidable Colonel Kennedy Shaw, look on with expressions of approval.

In 1930 the lease of Manor Farm was taken over by a widow, Ada Crouch, and her two dynamic sons, William and Robert. By all accounts she was a martinet and the two boys dynamos. Between them they took the farm by the scruff of the neck and dragged it into the 20th century, using all the latest technology, including mechanization and chemical fertilizers. In 1931 they bought their first tractor, and by the middle of the decade they had half a dozen. In 1933 they bought one of the first 'International' combine harvesters to be imported from the United States. It was the first one to be used in Wiltshire. A huge machine, it required 3 men to drive it, but it proved a tremendous saving in labour.

It is an irony that when as a consequence of the minimum wage regulations, the agricultural worker was, for the first time ever, marginally above the poverty line, he was being priced out of the market. Since the Crouches ran a mixed farm with other labour-intensive activities, they still employed a large workforce. However, with the introduction of their combine harvester, they had stepped on the slippery slope towards total farm mechanisation.

Against all the odds, the Crouches turned the farm into a profitable enterprise. The character of the

Frank Hardiman demonstrating a seed drill to Lady Bledisloe and Colonel Kennedy Shaw.

Bill Crouch of Manor Farm, Terffont Magna.

brothers—inventive, opportunistic and shrewd—undoubtedly contributed to their success. When the traditionally grown long-stalked wheat tended to choke the machine, Bob Crouch, in conjunction with the seed merchants, Dunns of Salisbury, set about breeding a short-stemmed variety, 'Vilmorin 27'. This solved the problem, but as a result, the straw—on which the village had relied for generations for thatching their roofs—was no longer usable for that purpose.

Bill, the other brother, managed to establish a cheap supply of pig-food by cornering the entire output of swill in Fovant, and he was quick to recognize that the bodies of some derelict gliders going for a song could easily be converted into coops for the expanding poultry flock.

The reputation achieved by the farm is illustrated by an event which occurred a few days before Christmas in 1939. A chauffeur arrived at the gate and announced that his mistress—who remained in the car—required a 28lb turkey. He was told that it was quite impossible, since all the birds were already sold. When the identity of the lady was revealed, however, it was found that there was, after all, a suitable bird left—for it was Queen Mary (the mother of the king).

In 1941, shortly after their mother's death, the Crouch brothers split up. Bob went into politics, while Bill took over the farm. He continued to prosper. Every Christmas until her death he presented Queen Mary with a turkey, and was rewarded on each occasion by being invited to tea with her.

Another successful village entrepreneur—albeit on a smaller scale—was Arthur Cox (whose daughter, Hilda Coombes, still lives in Tisbury). In order to escape from living in a tied farm cottage, under constant fear of being evicted, he acquired a piece of land on The Street in Teffont Magna and there erected a hut, which be bought in Fovant, and turned it into a house. He started off by raising poultry, and then moved on to pigs and dairy cattle. He set up a shop where he sold his own products, including home-cured bacon, and introduced the first milk round in the village by filling his customers' jugs from buckets carried on his bicycle. He prospered to the extent that in addition to owning a small but very productive farm, he was eventually able to buy extra land and build two bungalows on it.

An early tractor on Manor farm, Teffont Magna.

In 1922 Teffont Magna chapel had

Bill Crouch's tractors outside Manor Farm barn in the early 1930s.

been separated from its mother church in Dinton. If, however, the parishioners had hoped that they were being given independence, they were disappointed, for it was designated a chapelry of Teffont Evias. The most they could hope for was posthumous independence, since they were finally given their own graveyard, which was consecrated in 1925. When, however, the Reverend William Keatinge-Clay was appointed rector of the two churches (with a combined living of £400) in 1929, the two congregations became united in their high regard for him.

Three men still living today were young boys in Teffont in the early 1930s and retain clear memories of the time. The youngest of the three, Paffard Keatinge-Clay, was the rector's son. His clearest memories are of accompanying his father on visits to needy parishioners living in dark, dank cottages, and having nightmares after watching the gruesome charades acted by a visiting team of mummers. His more pleasurable recollections include walks beyond the village with his mother, when he was already appreciating the scene through the eyes of the artist he was to become. He had no real friends in the village; his mother discouraged him from associating with the local boys, for she had the impression that they were dirty.

No doubt she was often justified. Although their mothers took pains to see that their sons were clean when they went to school, when they were out playing it was a different matter. One of the boys, Bill Goodfellow, clearly remembers going home plastered in mud, being pushed into the stream and scrubbed by his mother before being let back into the house. It was fortunate that there was a handy stream outside the door, since taking a bath was not a simple matter. It involved carrying water in from a stand-pipe, heating it up in a copper, and then taking it by the bucketful to fill a tin bath placed on the kitchen floor. It was therefore a luxury rarely indulged in more than once a week. For the same reason, the washing of clothes was confined to once a week, always—rain or shine—on a Monday. The villagers took great pride in the quality of their laundry. Whites were boiled until they were like driven snow. It is not known if anyone was still using the 'receipt for soap to wash coloured linens', recorded in a 19th-century book of local village domestic tips, which recommended boiling up an ox gall with three pounds of white soap.

Arrangements for personal hygiene were probably not much more sophisticated in the rectory, but at least there were servants to carry the buckets of water. Paffard Keatinge-Clay records how he and his sister were forced to take a dip in the pond at the bottom of the garden every morning throughout the year. But this was in the interests of their health, rather than their cleanliness—or godliness.

The third of the boys mentioned was Frank Hardiman's son, Bill. Despite the fact that his family were not well off (he himself was glad to take a job looking after the farmer's chickens for 1s 6d a week), he remembers his youth as a time of great pleasure. That pleasure was shared by many other boys in the village, including Bill Goodfellow. His father, Vic, worked as a stockman for Colonel Kennedy Shaw, and is reputed to have been the best poacher in Wiltshire.

The rector took a great interest in the boys, training them in various sports, including football and boxing (although not on Sundays, when singing in the church choir for morning and afternoon services was de rigueur.) He also set up the first Scout troop in Teffont, and introduced the boys to the adventures of camping. Sunday School outings were another treat which the rector organized. They were exciting for children and parents alike, for few of them had ever travelled further afield than Salisbury.

These events took place during the summer, of course—a time when living in Teffont was enjoyable for all the village, when cottage doors could be left open and everyone was kept warm by the sun. Like the squirrels in their gardens, however, the more prudent of the villagers made preparations for winter, paying 6d a month into a coal club, to ease the financial burden when the cold days returned.

From 1931 to 1933 the poet Siegfried Sassoon lived in Fitz House. He was a close friend of Edith Olivier, and she often came to visit him there, as well as other members of their set: Rex and Laurence Whistler, Cecil Beaton and William Walton—all still struggling to find fame and fortune. It was a difficult time for Sassoon; his long relationship with Stephen Tennant had just ended, leaving him bitter and depressed. However, he eventually found consolation in the arms of one of Edith Olivier's young women friends, Hester Gatty. They became engaged while he was still living in Fitz House.

The Reverend Keatinge-Clay with his scout troop, including Paffard Keatinge-Clay (bottom right) and Bill Hardiman (top left).

Some of the conveniences of modern life were slowly finding their way to the village. Electricity was laid on in 1932. Those who could afford the rental were able to experience the miracle of switching on a clear, bright light in place of the smelly, smoky paraffin lamps. However, for many of the villagers, the oil lamp remained the source of light for a long time to come.

The credit for bringing electric light to the village was to some extent due to a resident of Teffont Evias: Gerald Keatinge's brother-in-law, Alexander Trotter. He had been one of the early pioneers of illumination by electricity, and has sometimes been referred to as the Newton of the electrical industry. For many years he was the Electrical Adviser to the Board of Trade.

A charabanc outing to Bournemouth in 1925.

In 1936 Teffont Evias and Teffont Magna were officially joined together as one parish with the name of Teffont. But it was no more than a marriage of convenience. The two villages continued along their separate tracks. One of the institutions which united them, Teffont Magna elementary school (which took children from both the communities), was closed down the same year.

Once a year, however, the two villages were drawn together for that great event: the annual Flower Show. The fact that it took place suggests a certain degree of luxury in the villagers' lives. They were prepared to devote space in their gardens to growing flowers as well as fruit and vegetables. In addition to flowers, there were classes of vegetables, home made bread, cakes and preserves, just as there are in our Village Show today, but the competition was hotter, often reflecting village rivalry. There was, however, one class no longer seen on the exhibitors' tables: rats' tails. In 1939 it was won by J Goddard, with an impressive bunch of 400 tails.

Rats were a terrible menace on the farms. They were kept out of some of the grain-stores by means of building them on the staddle stones which we now keep as ornaments in our gardens. But it was virtually impossible to keep them out of the barns.

Some time in 1934 the Honourable David Tennant drove through Teffont Evias and decided he wanted the manor. A highly successful entrepreneur, the proprietor of The Gargoyle (London's most prestigious club) and husband of the glamorous actress Hermione Baddeley, he was accustomed to getting what he wanted. He was therefore disconcerted when Gerald Keatinge refused to sell it to him. However, he reconciled himself to taking out a lease on it, especially since he was allowed to undertake a number of renovations, including installing plumbing. A few months later he and Hermione moved in, together with a cook, a butler, 5 maids, a 'boots', a governess, a nanny, and a chauffeur for his four cars. Alice Lee was sometimes called in to wait at table.

The Tennants may have flaunted their wealth, but they brought glamour and fun to the village. They had many riotous parties, chiefly for their private guests, who included some of the well-known actors of the day, including Lawrence Olivier. People who remember them still shake their heads and chuckle over the goings-on at these parties. Young Bill Goodfellow was astonished to see Hermione and her friends go skinny-dipping in the pool in the garden. From time to time the Tennants also gave parties for the villagers, and when they did so, they really pushed the boat out. Bill Hardiman remembers them well: dancing and laughter, tables groaning with food—and barrels of beer strategically placed along the hedges, so that nobody was ever short of a drink.

But David Tennant eventually grew tired of entertaining what he described as Hermione's 'crowd of mummers' every weekend. In 1936 they split up, and he married Virginia Parsons. From then on the manor was a rather quieter place. This must have been a relief to Gerald Keatinge, who had suffered a sad bereavement in 1935 when his beloved wife, Polly, died. He continued to live in Goldens and the Tennants to rent the manor until 1939. Although David Tennant was not the Keatinges' favourite tenant, he left behind one legacy which they appreciated: hundreds of crocus and daffodil bulbs in the garden, which went on flowering for many years. Virginia subsequently divorced the wayward David, and eventually returned to live not far away from Teffont as the Marchioness of Bath.

Gerald Keatinge could expect few favours—and the village little fun—from the next tenants to move into the manor. For it was the autumn of 1939: the war had begun, and the manor was requisitioned by the War Office.

The last day at Teffont school before its closure in 1936.

CHAPTER THIRTEEN

THE STREAM

The Second World War was different from all previous wars in its effects on the country (at least since the Norman Conquest), since it involved the entire population. Once the Declaration of War was made on 3 September 1939, nobody doubted that Britain would become the target of Hitler's bombers. Sirens were hastily installed to give warning of the approach of enemy aeroplanes, and gas masks were distributed to every man, woman and child.

Country towns and villages were regarded as being comparatively safe from deliberate bombing, but the area around Chilmark, including Teffont, was not considered safe enough to receive evacuees, since the old limestone quarries were being used by the military as an ammunition dump. The authorities were a bit sensitive about the situation. On one occasion a farm worker innocently ploughing a field was picked up by the police, since a reconnaissance plane had observed that he was driving his machine towards the corner of a field, which pointed towards the dump. It was in fact the logical direction in which to plough the irregularly-shaped field, but the fact that the ploughman was a conscientious objector perhaps made him more suspect.

A strict nightly blackout was enforced; all windows had to be fitted with thick curtains or screens. (The cottage-dwellers were probably glad they had the small windows which Paffard Keatinge-Clay had found so depressing). Friends and neighbours were now transformed into officious air-raid wardens, capable of shouting abuse at anyone failing to extinguish the light before opening the door to let the cat out. The Chairman of Teffont's Civil Defence Committee was Lord Bledisloe's agent, Colonel Kennedy Shaw—who, one can imagine, was in his element. His lieutenants were Gerald Keatinge, Bob Crouch, Charlie Giles and Bill Coombes.

Although there were no direct attacks on the country during the first 9 months of the war, the nation waited with horror as the German army rolled through France and the Low Countries in 1940. Teffont was able to gain first-hand experience of the British Army's defeat when some of the survivors evacuated from Dunkirk were found temporary billets in the old schoolhouse and the manor buildings. The villagers did what they could to help by providing accommodation for the wives and relatives of the soldiers.

During the months which followed—the time of the Battle of Britain—the village experienced many air-raid warnings, and Julia Giles, at school in Dinton, spent long periods in the school's air-raid shelter. But this was the result of German bombers flying over on their way to attack more worthwhile targets. In March 1941 a German bomber crashed into Dinton woods, causing great excitement.

This was the time of the greatest danger for the British Isles, when an invasion attempt by the Germans was thought to be imminent. The friendly countryside suddenly changed into an unfamiliar land where all sign-posts and place-names had been removed, and any stranger asking the way might well be an enemy agent. The villagers could no longer feel secure even in their own homes. The proclamation headed 'INVASION!!!' may read like an extract from a script for 'Dad's Army', but it was no joke to the villagers. The opening sentence: 'It is probable that England may be invaded at any moment ...' must have sent shivers down even the brawniest labourer's spine, and the advice that casualties would be dealt with 'as far as possible' by the First-Aid detachment, or that a hose and motor pump were being kept in Mr Giles' barn, cannot have brought great reassurance.

A platoon of Home Guard had been formed to defend the village. But at this time they had little more than their undoubted courage to offer as resistance to an enemy. There was only one rifle between six men.

In June 1941, Hitler sent his armies off to the Russian front, and so the threat of invasion of the United Kingdom was lifted. The bombing of major cities continued, but mainly at night. One night

The Teffont Home Guard, equipped with rifles. Left to right: Jack Goddard, Jack Lee, Reg Ashley, George Penny, Bill Hardiman, Ron Lever.

three bombs were dropped around the village. None did any serious damage, but the situation might have been very different if one of them—which weighed a ton and a quarter—had not failed to explode. It was an isolated occurrence, probably the result of random unloading—or perhaps some lonely shepherd had inadvertently put a match to his pipe.

It was a time when it was better to be a country mouse than a town mouse. Not only was there less risk of being bombed; there was also more food around. Rationing was as strict in the country as in the town, but the villagers had the produce of their gardens—and often allotments—to supplement their rations. Ironically, the poor were relatively less affected than the rich, since their food had long been rationed by their purses. Offal and rabbits—almost the only meat the farm labourer had ever been able to afford—were unrationed, and the allowance of two ounces of butter a week would have been a rare extravagance. Farm workers were allowed extra rations, especially at harvest time.

One of the refugees who came to the village to escape the bombing in London was Evelyn Buckton. She had bought a house in Teffont (which she named Wrens Nest—now Wrens Cottage) in 1927. However, her career as an artist required her to spend most of her time until the war travelling or working in her studio in Hampstead. She may have felt restricted during the years when the war obliged her to remain in Teffont, but she produced a number of beautiful watercolours and etchings of the village and surrounding countryside. She apparently smoked a pipe to keep the insects away when she was painting in the fields.

Enderley, Teffont Evias, before the iron railings were donated to the war effort.

INVASION !!!

1. It is probable that England may be invaded at any moment especially if the German war in Russia is successful. Remember the fall of France was chiefly due to the roads being blocked by the civil population which prevented the movement of troops. Therefore, if invasion comes, STAY PUT. You will be much safer in your own house, even if there is fighting taking place all round it, than you would be on the roads where you may be machine-gunned from the air. You may see frightened people on the roads pouring out of other places. Do not panic but show your sense by not joining them.

2. As the village may be entirely cut off by road, the Rural District Council have appointed a civil defence committee for each parish, to deal with emergencies and with the feeding of the population if supplies cannot get through. The members of the Teffont Committee are Colonel Kennedy Shaw and Messrs. G. Keating, R. F. Crouch, C. Giles and W. Combes.

3. If the village water mains are broken, do not drink the river water without boiling it. It would be better to get your drinking water at Springhead.

4. Casualities will be dealt with at Fitz House as far as possible, by the First-aid detachment.

5. In the event of fire, the motor pump and hose are kept in Mr. Giles' barn at Fitz Farm and Messrs. Roy Hannam and Loud are in charge of them.

6. If fires are started in the corn fields before harvest all able-bodied persons are expected to turn out and help to beat them out and save their own bread. Messrs. Crouch, Giles, Spencer and Burrows will have fire beaters ready.

7. If invasion begins, ALWAYS CARRY YOUR GAS MASK with you and practice wearing it at home beforehand. Your life may depend on this.

8. It is quite likely that enemy action or military traffic may prevent food supplies by road getting to the village. If so, the committee will do their best to feed everyone and you can help them most by making the best of things.

(Signed) F. S. KENNEDY SHAW,
Chairman, Teffont civil defence committee.

So far as farming was concerned, there was an almost exact repetition of what had taken place at the outset of the 1914-18 war. At the beginning of 1939 agriculture was in a state of acute depression, largely due to the import of low-priced grain and meat, but, as the year progressed, it became evident that the local product was going to be of vital importance. Methods of increasing soil fertility were discussed at a conference held at Teffont Evias Manor in June 1939, attended by 1,000 farmers. One of the principal speakers was Sir George Stapledon, an international authority on grassland ecology; the implementation of his farming methods are said to have contributed greatly to avoiding national starvation during the war. Sir George obviously took away a pleasant memory of the village, because many years later, when the manor had been converted into flats, he returned to live in one of them.

Farmers were ordered to cultivate every available acre of their land. Once again they found themselves with an increased workload, but since many of the farm workers had been called up, with an acute shortage of labour. This gap was eventually filled by 'land girls', members of the Women's Land Army, which Edith Olivier had helped to set up during the previous war. The sceptical local farmers discovered, to their surprise, that most of the girls were both skilled and efficient. While she was helping with the threshing, one of these girls, Cis Nairy, met the young man she would subsequently marry—young Bill Goodfellow. Eventually a few German prisoners of war were also brought in to give a hand in the fields.

At least the farmers had the consolation of knowing that there would be a ready market for everything they produced. As prices were strictly controlled, and farm labourers' minimum wages greatly increased (from 38s a week in 1939 to 60s in 1941), there was no opportunity for making big profits, but an efficient and enterprising farmer such as Bill Crouch could count on pulling in a decent living. In addition to his other farming activities, he established a market garden and sent his vegetables up on the train from Dinton to London, where they were in great demand.

Teffont Manor, showing the market garden.

At the end of 1941 the United States entered the war, and the following year, a detachment of the US 8th Air Force was posted to Teffont. Their encampment, mainly of Nissen huts, was spread around the village, for the most part on Gerald Keatinge's land. The US soldiers were generally regarded as welcome visitors, for they brought with them generous hearts and large supplies of wholesome food. Even their waste was a bonus, providing high-quality swill for the village pigs. Ministry of Food regulations limited the number of pigs slaughtered per annum to one per household.

However, as a result of the extra source of nourishment, the regulations were sometimes broken. Edith Giles had a narrow escape one day. A Ministry of Food inspector turned up just after she had killed two pigs (one undeclared). She managed to hide one carcass, but not the tub full of chitterlings from both animals. Fortunately the inspector swallowed her story that they had all been inside one remarkably large sow.

Sir Edgar and Lady Keatinge ('Kitty'), 1987.

The only people who had reservations about the presence of the US forces were the British soldiers billeted in Teffont Evias Manor. This became most apparent on Saturday nights, when dances were held in the Black Horse barn; even though girls came from as far away as Bristol, there were never enough to go round, and fights often broke out before the end of the evening.

Men from a series of British regiments were billeted in the manor and surrounding cottages: the Wiltshire Regiment, the Grenadier Guards, the Royal Artillery and finally the Royal Engineers. The latter were employed in printing maps of France in readiness for the invasion of Europe.

By 1944 Teffont was a part of the vast equipment park spread over much of southern Wiltshire, as preparations were made for the D-Day landings in June. The Ox Drove was concreted for several miles by the US forces to provide hard standing for tanks and supplies of ammunition.

The ageing Gerald Keatinge spent most of the war as a semi-recluse in Goldens, very likely watching with increasing dismay the deterioration of the manor in the hands of the military. When the war was over and the forces had moved out, Gerald's son, Edgar (later Sir Edgar), to whom he had made over the estate, came to Teffont with his wife, Kitty, to clear up the mess. They were prepared for the worst, as a soldier whom Kitty had nursed had told her how he and his friends had looted the lead tiles from the funny old manor house in Teffont where they were billeted, little realizing that she was the wife of the heir to the property. The Keatinges were able to obtain some compensation from the War Office and the US Air Force, but it was scarcely adequate.

It was the land rather than the buildings which caused them the greater heartache. Much of the woodland had been destroyed, and the gardens of the manor—described a few years earlier as 'a well-kept pleasance' with palms, tulip trees, limes, cedars and a rose garden—had been turned into a wasteland, dotted with patches of concrete and Nissen huts.

The cottages which had been requisitioned were also in bad repair, and some of them barely habitable. Kitty was shocked to discover that the majority of them still had no running water. (No doubt the soldiers would have been a bit taken aback too).

Home Farm was in an equally derelict condition. Despite Government directives to grow more food, Fred Spencer, the tenant farmer, appeared to have turned most of the land over to scrub. A part of the blame could perhaps have been put on the American forces, whose encampment spread over some of the arable land. Even so, Edgar lost no time in giving Spencer notice to quit. It took a long time to make the farm productive again.

The smaller Mill Farm, which was completely dairy, was in better shape. However, the tenant farmer, Ernest Horrell, left in 1946 to emigrate to Australia. Edgar did not replace him, but placed the herd in the charge of Horrell's competent dairyman, George Penny. As a consequence, the Pennys were invited to move into the spacious Mill farmhouse.

HARVEST 1948
MANOR FARM TEFFONT
AUGUST RAINFALL 5.51 INCHES
4 FINE DAYS
SEPT RAINFALL 6.52 INCHES
6 FINE DAYS
TERRIFIC GALES SWEEP THE
EARS OF CORN OFF THE STRAW
&
BEAUTIFUL CROPS VANISH &
RETURN TO MOTHER EARTH
BREAD IS RATIONED
MAY ALMIGHTY GOD
BLESS MANOR FARM AND ALL
WHO WORK WITHIN ITS CIRCLE
AND FOREVER SPARE THEIR
EYES FROM SUCH A DREADFUL
AND AFFECTING SIGHT
WFC

Inscription left by Bill Crouch to record the disastrous harvest in 1948.

Having spent the last four years cooped up with their two small boys in a two-room cottage rented for 2s 6d per week from Colonel Kennedy Shaw, the Pennys were more than happy to move, even though furnishing and running such a large house was not easy on a dairyman's wage. Also, it meant a lot of hard work for Gwen Penny, since in addition to keeping house, she had to help on the farm, where the nearest thing to mechanization was a creaking wheelbarrow. Life was complicated by the fact that the railway line ran between the dairy and the meadows, so that each time the cows were taken out to grass or brought back to milk, the guard had to be summoned to open the gates. Gwen remembers those early years for the relentless hard work, combined with the joy of being able to raise her children in such idyllic surroundings.

Teffont Magna had been left in better shape. The only scars on the landscape were on Manor Farm, where the US forces had turned one of the fields into a camp-site. But Bill Crouch with his customary acumen found a buyer for the Nissen huts.

The early post-war years were not easy ones. The country had regained peace, but not prosperity. Rationing was more severe than ever, and conditions were exacerbated by the disastrous summer of 1948—recorded so poignantly by Bill Crouch—when the harvest was completely ruined. With no American servicemen to help out with food and swill, it was a hungry time for the pigs as well as the villagers.

Teffont war memorial beside Teffont Magna church.

The end of the war meant that people could hand in their hated gas masks. Robert Baker, however, kept his and found a good use for it. He worked for Bill Crouch, and when Bill went in for indoor mushroom cultivation, Baker was given the job of spraying them. So noxious were the pesticides that Robert resorted to wearing his gas mask.

The character of the village began to change. Fortunately, there had been few casualties among those who went off to the war. The only ones not to return home were Lieutenant Martin Willan, Flight Sergeant R F Tinham, Gunner J M F Faramus, Private F W Wright and Private J Brockway. The demobilized servicemen and women, however, were less willing than before the war to work for a pittance as farm labourers or domestic servants. As a consequence the farmers made further endeavours to cut back their labour force by increasing mechanization. As a result of introducing mechanical milking, Charlie Giles could manage his farm with just three or four men.

Edgar Keatinge, however, was not highly mechanized, and he employed a dozen or so men on his estate and farm. One of them was a young man named Michael Faramus. His father had been groom to General Arnold Schreiber (later General Officer Commanding,Western Command), but while exercising the General's horse he had been killed by a falling tree. Michael's mother had stayed on in Teffont Evias, and, as soon as he left school, Michael went to work on the estate. He recalls that one of his tasks was to help replant the woods, which the US soldiers had cut down to erect their Nissen huts. They had left behind thick concrete bases, through which holes had to be blasted in order to plant the trees.

One of the most remarkable characters living in Teffont Magna at this time was a young man named Ron Lever. The son of a farm worker, he had been forced to leave school at fourteen and be apprenticed to a carpenter. He mastered his trade so well that within a few years he was established as the village carpenter and wheelwright, eventually taking on the additional roles of undertaker and general builder. But what made him really remarkable is that after leaving school with little more history knowledge than the names of the kings and queens of England, he became an expert in local and ancient history and a competent archaeologist. He had other accomplishments besides: apparently he could charm the birds off the trees and steal all the girls' hearts.

Already, in the years before the war, G H Engleheart, R S Newall and Colonel Kennedy Shaw had carried out excavations around the village and unearthed Roman remains and artefacts. Ron Lever followed in their footsteps. His enthusiasm may have been kindled by the discovery of a piece of Saxon carved stone while doing repairs to the church. Subsequently, rather than flirting with the girls he devoted his spare time to searching for further treasures, often in the old Teffont quarries, where he found artefacts ranging from Neolithic flints to Anglo-Saxon pottery sherds. His casual method of working, like that of his predecessors, would have been frowned upon today, especially since they did not trouble to make too many notes. But amateur archaeology was less regulated at that time, and as a result we have evidence of previous occupants of our village which might otherwise never have been uncovered.

At the same time John Thatcher, who owned Ley Farm, was making interesting discoveries on his land. His fields were so stony that he had to use a special plough on them, but among the stones were Mesolithic and Neolithic flints. He collected more than a thousand of them. Most were waste flakes, but a few were especially fine examples of Mesolithic craft.

In 1952 Teffont Magna came under the hammer again. The buyer was Lord Astor, but he sold it a few months later to the tenants he had acquired with it. The village was consequently almost completely divided between Bill Crouch's 1145-acre farm and Charlie Giles's 220 acres, although a few of the smaller tenants succeeded in buying their houses. For the first time in its history the village was owned by the people who actually lived there.

Ron Lever, aged seventy-four.

According to the memories of people still living, the late 1950s and early 1960s were the best years to live in the Teffonts. It was a time when they had a taste of modern life, but still enjoyed the flavour of the old.

They had electricity and running water (water mains were installed in the village in 1963). There were still two general stores, a post office, a pub and an excellent market garden (established by Sir Edgar Keatinge); a butcher, a baker, a fishmonger and even an ice-cream vendor paid regular visits. In addition, there was a petrol-pump in Teffont Evias not far from the blacksmith's shop. But few people possessed cars. Why should they need them? A bicycle was adequate for as far as most people wanted to go, and there was a regular bus service into Salisbury on market days.

The character of the Teffonts had not greatly changed; it was still rooted in the land. There were newcomers in the bigger houses, but the majority of the residents were still farm employees, and they enjoyed a great sense of community. They worked hard: the men six long days a week on the farms, and the women—with few modern conveniences and many mouths to feed—probably not much less. They had little leisure and not much money. Perhaps it was for this reason that they treasured and enjoyed to the full the little they had.

Gwen Penny remembers fine summer Sundays when as many as sixty people would join them for a picnic and a bathe in the river near the Mill. Then there was the Flower Show, which everyone prepared for and looked forward to with such relish. There was great fun bowling for pigs, and keen competition for the cups awarded for the best home-made jams and pickles and garden produce—but no more rats' tails!

In 1947 two distinguished nurses retired to Teffont: Miss Blyde and Miss Otley. They both left enduring memories: Miss Otley for her infinite kindness and Miss Blyde for her tireless zeal. In 1949 she set up a branch of the Women's Institute in Teffont, which in the same year compiled a history of the village. Conscientiously researched and beautifully hand-written, with watercolour and pen-and-ink illustrations, it demonstrates that the village women were capable of more sophisticated activities than making jam and organizing whist-drives when given the opportunity.

The Teffont Women's Institute had forty-four members when they produced the history, many of them descendants of old village families. But there were some newcomers. One of these was Margery Lancaster-Rankin, who with her husband had moved into the Malt House on their return from India at the end of the war.

It was fortunate that they had brought a large number of packing cases with them. The Malt House was a bit run down, and building materials were scarce. So Major-General Lancaster-Rankin used the wood from tea-chests to replace floor-boards, and the packing cases to construct cupboards. Years later, shelves were discovered with Poonah labels on them. Many cupboards were needed to store Margery's extensive collection of exotic clothes. She was a colourful personality in every sense, still fondly remembered for her warmth and generosity.

Another returning soldier, Lieutenant Colonel Evan Nepean, brought his wife Cicily and their daughters to live in Teffont Evias in 1947. Although he was the heir to a baronetcy, and there were whole streets or districts bearing the name 'Nepean' in Ottawa, Melbourne and Bombay in memory of his great great-grandfather, the profligacy of certain of his forebears had deprived Evan of an ancestral home in England. His great passion in life was radio. As a young Signals Officer in 1936 he had been sent to Lhasa with the British Political Mission led by Basil Gould to provide communications. He and his fellow Signals Officer, Sydney Dagg, were obliged virtually to invent a wireless set capable of transmitting messages back to Delhi. Sixty years later—until shortly before his death—Sir Evan was using a not

Howards House and its garden, which was restored in 1948.

dissimilar machine to communicate with other amateur radio enthusiasts throughout the world.

In 1952 Major and Mrs Mordaunt-Hare acquired Fitz House. It was still subject to the problems Edith Olivier had suffered, with 2 inches of water in one of the downstairs rooms when they first saw it. However, they were eventually able to rectify the matter, and were then able to turn their attention to the garden and to build on the foundations which French had created. With Vita Sackville-West as their inspiration, they planted a profusion of flowering plants, especially clematis and roses.

Back in 1947 Kitty Keatinge might also have been found working in a garden, the one created by Henry Howard. Having decided that the manor had outgrown its use as a single residence, the Keatinges were in the course of converting it into three flats and had moved into Howard's House. This had also been occupied by the army throughout the war. As a result, Howard's pride and joy had turned into a bramble patch, so thick, Kitty indignantly recorded, that the fish pond was completely obscured, and she fell into it. Walter Coombes was put in charge of the garden's restoration, but it was a hard task, even with a team of German prisoners-of-war to help him.

The first occupant of one of the manor house flats was Alexander Trotter's widow, Alys, a talented sculptress and poet. She lived until she was a hundred years old, and organized the annual Poppy Day appeal until she was ninety-six.

Bringing up children in Teffont during the fifties and sixties presented fewer problems than today. They had few toys, but an immense playground. They could gambol in the meadows, run races along the Ox Drove, play hide-and-seek in the woods, cycle along the lanes, fly kites from the common, fish and swim in the river or chat up Ron Lever in his workshop, all without fear or restraint.

Almost the only organized entertainment was provided by the rector, Reverend Bernard Briggs. Like Keatinge-Clay, Reverend Briggs devoted much time to pastoral care, and especially to the village children. He held a weekly youth-club meeting at his house, which was not the splendid old rectory where Keatinge-Clay had lived, but a more modest and easily-run house not far from the Black Horse. The old rectory was now a private residence called Bridges, which had been bought in 1937 by Brigadier Hugh Willan and his wife.

Amongst other activities for the young of the village, the Reverend Briggs provided an old Rolls Royce (which he had bought for £1) for them to take to pieces, in order to learn about the workings of a car.

He encouraged the village football team, at that time twenty strong, and when Southampton were playing at home, he would cram as many young football fans as possible into the back of his van and take them down to watch the match. The Teffont team became sufficiently well organised by the early 1970s to take part in tournaments arranged for small teams in Europe. For several years in succession Bill Goodfellow led them off to play matches in France, Belgium, Germany and Spain.

Walter Coombes and his wife in Howards House garden.

In 1960, shortly after Brigadier Willan's death, his son, Group-Captain Andrew, returned with his wife, Joan, to take over Bridges, which had become the Willan family home. They both settled easily into country life. Andrew, a World War II bomber pilot, who had been shot down over France in 1941 and forced to spend the remainder of the war in prison camps, went into local politics, eventually becoming Chairman of Wiltshire County Council and a Deputy Lieutenant of Wiltshire. Joan, the daughter of an Oxford don, busied herself with village affairs and gardening, becoming a great authority on garden plants.

Joan was typical of the women of her generation who lived in the country. Although they were nearly all capable of more intellectual activities, they found fulfilment in a life of domesticity, combined with simple country pursuits: walking their dogs, searching for rare wild flowers, watching birds (among which skylarks, nightingales, corncrakes and nightjars could still be seen in the vicinity of Teffont), organizing fetes, and gardening—especially gardening. Had these women been young today, they would most likely have sought more stimulating occupations. As a result, the village would have been denied some of its most beautiful gardens.

The first prize for gardening must go to Gill Mordaunt-Hare. With the help of her husband (it must be said), she created an outstanding garden at Fitz House. It was featured in 'Country Life' in 1990, and was open to the public from 1983 to 1993. People came from far and wide to visit it.

I would also like to award a consolation prize to Alice Lee's brother, Jack, the results of whose work can be seen every year in the early spring when the bank of the road opposite Teffont Evias church becomes carpeted with the snowdrops which he planted. He is still remembered for his kindness as well as his gardening skill.

In 1960 Bill Crouch received the accolade he had always coveted: the Royal Warrant awarded to him by Queen Elizabeth, the Queen Mother, for his turkeys. Three years later he retired and sold the farm. He had had a remarkable career, prospering through bad times as well as good. He was a shrewd businessman, but a generous friend to the village. He could be counted on to put his hand in his pocket when Teffont Magna church was in need of expensive repairs. Moreover, while most farmers were scaling back their work-force, he kept 27 of the village men in employment.

But the days of mixed farming were clearly numbered. The buyers of Manor Farm, Alastair Pitcairn and his brother, Angus, concentrated on agrarian. They adopted the newly recommended practice of removing hedgerows to enlarge fields and facilitate ploughing. It was a much less labour-intensive type of farming, and they reduced the work force to seven men.

Dinton schoolchildren dancing on Teffont Manor lawn for the church fete in 1950. Ruth Bull is in the centre of the foreground.

Charlie Giles retired in 1967 and passed on his dairy farm to his daughter, Julia, and her husband, Francis Crossman. His retirement was, however, of short duration, for Francis died a few weeks later—killed by his own bull. It was not until eight years later, when Julia married John Vining, that Charlie was finally able to retire. His name has been given to the exhibition farm, 'Farmer Giles's Farmstead', which now occupies part of the land. Giles's granddaughter's husband, Paul Skelton, runs the remaining dairy/agrarian operation, with the help of one assistant, Peter Johnson, who holds the distinction of being the only agricultural worker left in the village.

In January 1982 Teffont was the scene of another tragic accident. Sheila Barr, wife of Douglas Barr, the Evias water bailiff, was returning home after walking her Alsatian dog, and went to cross the railway line near Teffont Mill. That is the last she remembers before regaining consciousness and finding that she had lost a leg. The fact that she was suffering from an inner ear disease, which affected her balance as well as her hearing, may well have contributed to the accident. Her beloved dog was killed outright.

When Brian Wilde took over the tenancy of Teffont Evias Home Farm in 1966 there were only five men left working on it. He was unable to keep on the market garden—so popular with village residents—because of competition from neighbouring 'pick-your-own fruit' nurseries, forcing him to deplete his workforce even further. He kept the dairy farm going until 1993, after which the pastures were used for beef cattle, and the work force was reduced to one person. After his retirement in 1999 the farm was leased to a farming complex based in Tisbury.

Ley Farm is still in operation in the hands of the Thatcher family in Great Wishford. Ten acres of the old Mill Farm is owned by Dr and Mrs Graham Miller, who run Jacob and Wiltshire Horn sheep, while giving the Teffont Fishing Club the right to use their stretch of the River Nadder. The Manor Farm in Teffont Magna has been divided up. The old farmyard is now an elegant livery stable, while most of the remainder is a combination of agrarian and pheasant/partridge shooting.

By the end of the 1970s lack of work had driven most of the agricultural workers from the village. Farm labour is obviously not the easiest way of earning a living, but many of them left their old cottages with regret. When they did so, they took from the village something of great importance: its raison d'être.

Superficially the village does not appear to have changed a great deal during the last century. It is still dominated by old stone cottages, many with thatched roofs, standing along the edge of the stream, looking little different from the time Paffard Keatinge-Clay visited them with his father. But their interiors have been completely transformed. They were not left empty for long after being vacated by the agricultural workers. They were taken over by a new breed of owners—retired people, or those wanting a country life. The old stone cottage had acquired a certain cachet, provided, of course, that it was suitably modernised inside.

Unfortunately for the village, the newcomers all had cars; so the local shops and the post office closed down through lack of business. There was no longer a need for a blacksmith, and eventually even the Black Horse closed its doors. An ever-increasing volume of traffic passes through the village, and an ever-decreasing number of pedestrians walk around it, severely reducing the chance of friendly encounters which were so much a part of old country life. Even when parked in the village, the cars still appear inappropriate—a complete incongruity against the age-old stone and thatch.

However, Teffont Manor looks little different from when it was John Mayne's seat, although the surrounding estate has been reduced. It is still in the ownership of the Keatinge family, who are his direct descendants. There are trees in the park planted by John Mayne, and swans still swim on Emily de Salis's lake. Glimpses of the old life can be seen just outside the village, where John Webb still keeps shire horses, and at Farmer Giles's Farmstead, where there is a collection of the old farming implements which Giles himself may well have used. And if the ghost of John Aubrey were to pass by, he would note that there is once again 'a pretty vineyard' in Teffont.

Although the old farming village has died, Teffont has found a new life. There is no longer the sense of community which there once was. In its place there is a loosely-knit society of individuals, with a deep attachment to the village, but with a wide range of personal interests. There is, as might be expected, a fair number of retired people, and also a scattering of commuters. What is surprising is the large number of small businesses now based in Teffont, ranging from organic horticulture to T-shirt printing. The old barn, once a part of the Black Horse Inn, is now the headquarters of The Francis Frith Collection (photographic publishers), and behind the neo-Georgian facade of Greystones is the office of Famous Fishing. The oldest business is Richard Bull's building firm, examples of whose enduring work may be seen throughout the village. In Wrens Cottage Pamela Fisher keeps alive the artistic tradition established by Evelyn Buckton, specializing in decorative flower arrangement and exotic costume-making, while in the rustic setting of Home Close, David Parker runs an efficient, modern printing and publishing operation. You may no longer be able to post a parcel in the village or fill up your car with petrol, but you can get your lawn-mower repaired and your antique furniture restored; you can consult an architect, buy a bottle of wine or an antiquarian book, and learn to ride a horse.

Engraving showing the River Nadder near Teffont Mill by Evelyn Buckton.
Courtesy of Pamela Fisher

Teffont Magna Manor Farmhouse as it is today.

The Black Horse Inn, a popular stopping-off point for travellers up until the end of the 20th century.

This change in the character of the village is just the latest of a long series, which began in the fifth millennium BC, when the Neolithic farmers replaced the Mesolithic hunters. The Neolithic, in their turn, were succeeded by the metal-workers, first the Bronze Age men who introduced mead, and subsequently the Iron Age people, who came with steely hearts as well as iron weapons. The Roman invaders changed life dramatically by pushing through a road, opening up the quarries and introducing currency. Under the Anglo-Saxon yoke, the villagers learned to serve one God but saw their territory split up between two different landlords. Then came the Normans, who set the feudal system in stone under their own more ruthless lords. So it continued: change after change. Some were brought about by calamities, such as the plague and civil wars. Others were due to economic influences, such as the rise and fall of the wool industry and the fluctuating market for corn. Finally, the mechanization of agriculture and lower demand for domestic products led inevitably to the demise of Teffont as a farming village.

One feature of the village which has suffered little change is the stream. Teffont owes not only its name, but its very existence to the spring of pure water which rises to the north of the village and flows through its heart. It was this which drew the very earliest settlers to the site, and subsequent inhabitants have, throughout the centuries, made use of its water for drinking, cooking, washing, and watering their animals and their meadows. Today, we regard it as an ornament rather than an amenity, enjoying its changes of mood, from serene and sparkling on summer days to rushing mini-torrent in winter. Occasionally it has flooded. The last time, still fresh in the memory of the village, was in 1999, when the stream was overwhelmed by topsoil from a pig farm swept into the valley by torrential rain. But for most of the time, the Teff stays well within its banks, tumbling gently towards the Nadder, as it has done since the beginning of the village's history.

Teffont during the floods of 1999.

A lot of water has flowed under the Teffont bridges since we began this project. It was only after we had embarked upon it that we appreciated the size of the task and the depth of history to be uncovered. Some of the events recorded above have taken place during the three years since it began. Newcomers have arrived, old residents have left; we have experienced the joy of new births and the sorrow of losing old friends. But this only indicates that history is an ongoing affair, which does not stop when you finish recording it.

A view of the village in 2003. (VK)

ACKNOWLEDGEMENTS

This history of Teffont owes a great deal to the villagers of Teffont, who gave generous support to the project, undertaking researches, supplying personal information, ransacking their minds for old memories and their attics for old photographs.

We are especially indebted to Pamela Fisher, who accumulated much of the information used in the chapters concerning the 20th century; to the late Lady Keatinge, whose unpublished history of Teffont Evias Manor provided invaluable background material, and to her son, Bill Keatinge, for allowing us access to his family's private papers. Invaluable help and information has also been provided by James Crouch, Bill Hardiman, Ruth Bull, Michael Faramus, Alice Lee, Cis and Bill Goodfellow, Clifford Lever, Margaret Foy, Diana Jefford, Gwen Penny, Felicity and Tony Little, David Parker, Callie Troup, Margaret and David Briggs, Violet Hoare, Ann Ashton, Sue Nicoll, Barbara Baker, Cicily Nepean, Brian Wilde, Sara Willan, Noele Thompson, Joan Parsons, Hilda and David Coombes, Julie and John Vining, Joan and Tom Thatcher, Brian Sarginson, Kathleen Merrifield, Josephine Fulford, Betty Wrixon, John Webb, Carolyn Mabey, Jasper Bascon, and Joan and Jonathan Foster, all of whom contributed significantly towards our account of the village history. Paffard Keatinge-Clay, now living in Spain, kindly allowed us to quote from his memoirs.

We would also like to offer our thanks to the many people with no direct connections with the village who have helped us with material and information. These include Della Hooke, Peter Stannier, Martin Green, Burt Freeman, Ben Elliott, Alan Dodge, Mary James, Graham Sprackling of Evias Harold, Mark Bowden and other members of staff of English Heritage, Helena Cave Penny of Libraries and Heritage, Julie Gardiner and Andrew Fitzpatrick of Wessex Archaeology, Andrew Crookston and staff of Wiltshire Records Office, Andrew Deathe and Martin Wright of Salisbury Museum, Bruce Purvis, Eve Finlay and staff of Salisbury and Wilton branches of the Wiltshire County Library, Robert Lloyd and staff of English Nature, Devizes Museum and the Natural History Museum, London.

Two people to whom we also owe thanks are our husbands, St Elmo Nelson and Malcolm McBain, for their encouragement and good advice. Sadly, St Elmo did not live to see the publication of our history.

An especial vote of thanks is due to our generous sponsors:

John Buck, The Francis Frith Collection, Teffont
Tom Ashe Lockhart (in memory of Joan Willan)
Salisbury District Council

GLOSSARY

AGRICULTURAL

BANE: Sheep rot

BORDAR: Holder of small amount of land—5–15 acres with cottage—in exchange for menial services to lord

CASSATE: Measure of land—one hide.

COTTAR: Inhabitant of cottage, often without land.

CLOSE: Enclosed field.

COPYHOLD: Old system of holding land. Services due to the lord as condition for lease of land was entered on manor court roll, copy of which was given to the tenant.

DEMESNE: Land held by lord for his own use, cultivated by labour of tenants.

EINKORN: Ancient variety of wheat—grown in Neolithic period.

EMMER: Early species of wheat.

HECTARE: 100 ares (2.471 acres).

HERIOT: Fine due to lord of manor on death of tenant (often 'best beast').

HIDE: Flexible measurement, varying from 120 to 40 acres—basically as much land as could be tilled

by one plough in a year, or enough to sustain one family.

HUNDRED: 100 hides, subdivision of county, having its own court.

PANNAGE: Feeding swine on beech-mast, acorns etc. in forest.

SERF: Person bonded in servitude to the lord.

STRIP FIELDS: Unenclosed fields, comprising strips each 1 furlong in length and 1 acre in area—amount of land a team of oxen could plough in one day.

THREE-FIELD SYSTEM: Yearly rotation of fields: one sown with wheat, one sown with barley, one left fallow.

THEGN: Anglo-Saxon nobleman, holding land with service obligation to king.

VILLEIN: (at time of Domesday book), holder of statutary amount of land, usually around 30 acres, with rights in the common meadow and pasture, but bound to render services to lord as condition of holding land.

VIRGATE: Fourth part of hide.

YEOMAN: Freeholder below the rank of gentleman.

ARCHAEOLOGICAL

AMMONITE: Fossil marine animal with coiled shell, resembling snail.

ADZE:Cutting tool with blade set at right-angles to the handle.

BELEMNITE: Pointed fossil—internal shell of mollusc.

BIVALVE: Animal with shell in two valves or parts.

BURIN: Chisel-shaped flint tool.

CORE: Lump of stone remaining after flakes have been struck off it.

HORSHAM POINT: Minute microlith of later Mesolithic period.

HYPOCAUST: Roman heating system.

ICHTHYOSAUR: Extinct marine reptile similar to dolphin.

KNAPPER: Flint cutter.

OSTRACOD: Minute fossil crustacean with bivalve shell.

PLIOSAUR: Giant marine reptile.

POT BOILER: Pebble heated and used to boil water.

POTSHERD: Fragment of pottery.

RUNIC: Ancient Celtic style of ornamental interlacing.

SARSEN: Grey coloured, rounded block of hard sandstone found especially on Marlborough Downs.

TORC (TORQUE): Necklace or armband of twisted metal.

MISCELLANEOUS

(OLD MONEY—before the decimalization of currency in 1971)

d. penny or pence

s. shilling—equivalent of 12 pence.

£. pound, equivalent of 20s. or 240d.

BIBLIOGRAPHY

Documents

Church Wardens' Accounts, Teffont Magna from 1536, Teffont Evias, from 1804.
Census returns 1841, 1851, 1861, 1871, 1881, 1891, 1901.
NADFAS Record of Teffont Evias and Teffont Magna churches 1995.
Monthly assessment for Relief of Ireland 1648.
Pembroke Estate rent rolls.
Pembroke Surveys 1631-2.
Registers of Births, Deaths and Marriages.
Tithe Apportionment Map, Teffont Evias, 1840.
Women's Institute History Scrap-Book of Teffont, 1956.
Private documents in the possession of Professor W. Keatinge.

Printed Material

R.Anderton: A Dynamic Stratigraphy of the British Isles.
W.R.Andrews and A.J.Jukes-Browne: The Purbeck Beds of the Vale of Wardour.
(London Geological Society Journal, Vol 50).
Antiquaries Journal 1923: Surface Implements from Wiltshire.
J. Aubrey: Natural History of Wiltshire.
A.T.Bannister: History of Evias Harold.
S.Barker: The Practical Fossil Finder.
R.S.Barron: The Geology of Wiltshire.
N. Barton: Stone Age Britain.
A.Burl: Stonehenge People.
J.H.Bettey: Rural Life in Wessex; Wessex from 1,000 A.D.
R. Bewley: Book of Prehistoric Settlements.
W.P.S. Bingham: James Ley, Earl of Marlborough.
K. Branigan: Roman Britain.
British Museum: British Mesozoic Fossils.
P. Campion: A Recent History of Hampshire, Wiltshire and Dorset.
A.& F. Cayel (Eds.): Rolls of the Fifteenth—Lay Subsidy.
R.C.C. Clay: Flint Implements from the Nadder Valley. (W.A.M. No.43, 1968).
W.Churchill: History of the English Speaking People.
G.E.Cockayne: The Complete Peerage.
J. Collis: Iron Age in Wessex.
R. Colt Hoare: History of Ancient Wiltshire; History of Modern Wiltshire.
J.C. Cox: The Parish Churches of England.
A.Crane: Prehistoric Facts and Lists.
D.A. Crawley (Ed.): The Wiltshire Tax List 1332.
P. Cunnington: How Old is That Church?
B.Cunliffe: Ancient Celts; Danebury; Iron Age Britain; Wessex to A.D. 1,000.
E. Darby: A French Sculptor in Wiltshire. (W.A.N.H.M Vol 95).
H.C.Darby: Domesday England.
T.Davis: General View of the Agriculture of Wiltshire 1811.
Declarcon of Ley: The Ley Family of Teffont Ewyas, Wilts. (W.R.O.).
Dictionary of National Biography.
A.Dodge: Freshford.
J. & P. Drury: Tisbury History.
E.Duffy: The Voices of Morebath.
R. Ehrenreich: Iron Working in Iron Age Wessex.
M. Edmunds: Stone Tools in Society.
P. Ellis (Ed.): Roman Wiltshire and After.
J. Evans: The Environment of Early Man in the British Isles.
F.E.Farmer: English Historical Documents (c.500 –1042).
A.P. Fitzpatrick and E.Morris: The Changing Iron Age of Wessex.
A.P. Fitzpatrick and A.D. Crockett: A Romano-British Settlement and Inhumation Cemetery at Eyewell Farm, Chilmark. (W.A.M.H.) May 1998.
R.A. Fortey: The Hidden Landscape.
E. & C. Fry (Eds.): Abstracts of Wiltshire Inquisitions Post Mortem Charles I.
C. Gamble: The English Palaeolithic Reviewed.
I. Geddes: Hidden Depths.
C. Gingell and P. Harding: A Field Walking Survey in the Vale of Wardour (W.A.N.H.M. Vol 77).
G.E.B. Gover, A.Mawer, F.M.Stenton: Place Names of Wiltshire.
G.W. Green: The Geology of Building Stones in Dorset, Hants and Wilts. (Hatcher Review, Vol V. No. 45).
M. Green: A Landscape Revealed.
P. Harding and D.R. Bridgland: Pleistocene Deposits and Palaeolithic Implements at Godolphin School. (W.A.N.H.M. Vol 91).
A.C. Harfield: A History of the Village of Chilmark 1961.
D. Hinton: Alfred's Kingdom—Wessex and the South 800-1500.
D. Hooke: The Framework of Early Medieval Wessex.
W.H. Hudson: A Shepherd's Life.
J. Hunter & I. Ralston (Eds.): The Archaeology of Britain.
S. James: Exploring the World of the Celts.
S. Johnson: Later Roman Britain.
S.E. Kelly (Ed.): Charters of Shaftesbury Abbey.
Kelly's Directory (passim).
E. Kerridge (Ed.): Surveys of the Manors of Philip, First Earl of Pembroke.
J.L. Kirby (Ed.): Abstracts of Feet of Fines 1377-1509.
J.L. Kirby (Ed.): A Calendar of the Earl of Radnor's Cartulary of the Hungerford Family.
R. de C. Kivell: Romano-British Settlement at Stockton Earthworks (Wiltshire Magazine Dec. 1926.)

R. Lacey and D. Danziger (Eds.): The Julius Work Calendar, the year 1,000.
J. Laing: Warriors of the Dark Ages.
B. Lee: An Introduction to Geology.
T. Lever: The Herberts of Wilton House.
M. Luke: David Tennant and the Gargoyle Years.
T.MacLachlan: Civil War in Wilts.
D. McOmish: Settlement Patterns in the lst Millennium B.C.
D. McOmish, D. Field and G, Brown: Field Archaeology of the Salisbury Plain Training Area.
R.V. Melville and E.C. Freshway: British Regional Geology, The Hampshire Basin and Adjoining Areas, 4th ed.
M. Millet: Roman Britain.
R.J.Mitchell and D.R.Leys: A History of the English People.
F.W. Morgan: Woodland in Wiltshire at Time of Domesday Book.
T.Mowl: William Beckford.
J.W.G. Musty, D.A.L. Davies, J.R. Hunter, D. Morgan:
The Roman Road from Old Sarum to the Mendips—the Grovely Wood—Old Sarum Section.
National Trust: Mompesson House.
P. Parker: The Bronze Age.
J. Peddie: Invasion.
G.D. Ramsay (Ed.): Two 16th-Century Tax Lists, 1545 and 1576 (W.A.N.H. Sty.)
M. Ransome (Ed.): Wiltshire Returns to Bishop's
Visitation Queries 1783.
J. Richards: Stonehenge.
A.J. Ross and E.A. Garzembowski: A Provisional Checklist of Fossil Insects from the Purbeck Group of Wiltshire (W.A.N.H.M. Vol.89 1996).
P. Salway: Roman Britain.
Salisbury Journal (passim).
Salisbury and Winchester Journal (passim).
N. Saul: Historic Atlas of Britain, Pre-Historic to Medieval.
A.Savage (comp.): Anglo-Saxon Chronicles.
R. Sawyer: The Nadder: Tales of a Wiltshire Valley.
N. Sharples: Maiden Castle.
R. Skinner: Ley Family of Teffont Evias and Westbury and Earldom of Marlborough (W.A.N.H.M. 1998).
A.G.Street: Various works.
R.J. Small: Escarpment Dry Valleys of the Wiltshire Chalklands. (Institute British Geographies No. 34, June 1964).
G.D. Squibb (Ed.): Wiltshire Visitation Pedigrees 1623.
E. Stokes (Ed.): Abstracts from Wiltshire Inquisitions Post Mortem Edward III.
C.R. Straton: An Elizabethan Manor in the time of Elizabeth.
D. Sturdy: Alfred the Great.
W.E.Tate: The Parish Chest.
T. Tatton-Brown: The Building Stone for Salisbury
Cathedral (Hatcher Vol V, No.45).
C. & T. Thorn (Eds.): Domesday Book Wiltshire.
E.M.Trevelyan: Social History.
Victoria County History of Wiltshire (passim).
J. Wacher: The Coming of Rome.
R. Waller: The New Age.
Bruce Watkin: History of Wiltshire.
B. Welch: Geology of Wiltshire.
M. Welch: Anglo-Saxon England.
E.R. Welldon-Finn: An Introduction to the Domesday Book.
R. White: Memories of a Victorian Farmer.
R.Whitlock: A Lost Village; A Victorian Village.
Alfred Williams: In a Wiltshire Village.
Ann Williams (Ed. in chief): Domesday Book Studies (Alecto Hist. Studies 1987).
L.J. Wills: A Paleographical Atlas of the British Isles.
M. Wood: In Search of the Dark Ages.
J. Wroughton: An Unhappy Civil War.
J. Wymer: Lower Palaeolithic Occupation of Britain;
Mesolithic Britain; Three Hand Axes from Stapleford, Wiltshire. (W.A.N.H.M.)

ILLUSTRATIONS

Bracketed initials below photographs
PL - Peter Letcher L.R.P.S VK - Victoria Knowles EF - Eleanor Fisher
We would like to thank the above for the excellent photographs which they generously provided to illustrate our book. Our thanks are also due to the many members of the village who allowed us to reproduce their old and precious photographs.

CHAPTER HEADING ILLUSTRATIONS

The chapter heading illustrations are details from the Dutch medieval panels in Teffont Evias church. Reproduced by courtesy of Peter Letcher.

Chapter 1	David
Chapter 2	David slaying Goliath
Chapter 3	Hunting scene
Chapter 4	Hunting scene in forest
Chapter 5	Christ in Gethsemane
Chapter 6	Bishop reading book
Chapter 7	Soldiers firing muskets
Chapter 8	Soldier drawing sword
Chapter 9	Jesse and David
Chapter 10	Joseph and Isaac
Chapter 11	Armorial
Chapter 12	Huntsman
Chapter 13	Grotesque face representing the moon

TIMES OF FORMATION OF SURFACE ROCKS OF TEFFONT

Upper Portland	Jurassic
Lower Purbeck	Jurassic
Middle Purbeck	Jurassic
Upper Purbeck	Jurassic
Wealden	Cretaceous
Lower Greensand	Cretaceous
Gault	Cretaceous
Upper Greensand	Cretaceous
Lower Chalk	Cretaceous
Middle Chalk	Cretaceous
Upper Chalk	Cretaceous
Valley Gravel	Pleistocene/recent

GEOLOGICAL TIME CHART

Period	Approx no. of years ago
Devonian	395-345 million
Carboniferous	345-280 million
Permian	280-230 million
Triassic	230-195 million
Jurassic	195-141 million
Cretaceous	141- 65 million
Tertiary	65- 2 million
Quaternary	
(Pleistocene)	2 million-10,000
(Holocene)	10,000 - present

INDEX

Acacia Cottage, 94
Aethelgifu, 25
Aethelwolf, King, 24
Alfred (Alured), Baron of Marlborough, 27, 28, 29
Alfred, King, 24, 25
Alms-houses, 94
Ambrosius Aurelianus, 22
Andrews, Rev W H, 7
Arthur, 22
Ash, Jesse, 107
Ash, John II, 63
Ash, John Jr, 61, 62, 63, 64
Ashe, James, 59
Ashe, John II, 59, 60
Ashe, John, 57, 58
Astor, Lord, 120
Aubrey, John, 50, 53, 60
Avebury, 12
Baberstock, Walter, 53
Baberstock, William, 52, 53, 61
Baddeley, Hermione, 111, 112
Badon Hill, 22
Baker, Barbara, 99
Baker, Robert, 119
Barford, 8
Bathurst, Charles, Lord Bledisloe, 102, 104, 105, 107
Beaton, Cecil, 110
Beckford, William Jr, 69, 70, 76
Beckford, William Sr, 69
Bedwell, John, 68
Berkely, Hon Grantley, 83
Berwick St James, 14
Birinus, 25
Black Death, 35, 36
Black Horse inn, 53, 69, 75, 77, 93, 98, 103, 106, 117, 125, 126
Botreaux, Margaret, 39, 40
Briggs, Rev Bernard, 122
Brodie, Rev Peter, 7
Buckton, Evelyn, 115
Bugg family, 91
Bull, Harry, 101
Bull, Richard, 126
Butt, James, 70
Camelot, 22
Carolina, 63
Census: of 1841, 85, 87; of 1851, 89; of 1881, 93; of 1901, 98
Chaunders, John, 36
Chicksgrove, 64, 66, 81
Chilmark, 12, 53, 62, 63
Christianity, brought to Wessex, 25
Chubb, William, 85, 93
Church, Teffont Evias, 30, 32, 39, 46, 50, 55, 56, 64, 78, 79, 81, 82, 83, 84, 88, 95
Church, Teffont Magna, 30, 32, 38, 46, 76, 89, 108, 109
Churchwardens, 76, 77
Civil War, 54, 55
Clay, Dr G C, 10
Clos, Margaret, 66
Clubmen, 55
Cnut, King, 25
Coles, John, 91
Coombes, Bill, 113
Coombes, Daniel, 98, 107
Coombes, Hilda, 108
Coombes, Walter, 122
Corfe Castle, 26
Cottage, The, 82, 88, 106
Cox, Arthur, 108
Cox, William, 87
Crouch, Ada, 107
Crouch, Robert, 107, 108, 113
Crouch, William, 107, 108, 116, 118, 119, 120, 124
Crowther, Jane, 89
Dalwood mill, 29, 32, 38
Daniell family, 61
Davies, Richard, 87
Davis family, 66
Davis, Edward, 65
Daye House, The, 104
Dinton church, 44, 45, 47, 109
Dinton churchwardens' accounts, 44, 45, 48
Dinton, 25, 27, 32, 33, 36, 38, 44, 66, 78
Domesday Book, 27, 28
Drew, Edward, 91
Dyer, Bessie, 98
Edgar, King, 25
Edington, 24
Electricity laid on, 110, 111
Elsbury, 16
Engleheart, Rev G H, 10, 19, 120
Evias place-name meaning, 28
Ewyas Harold Castle, 28, 36
Eyewell, 20
Famous Fishing, 126
Faramus, Michael, 119
Farleigh Hungerford Castle, 37
Farmer Giles's Farmstead, 125
Farmer, William and Lavinia, 107
Farming: in Neolithic times, 12; in Iron Age, 16; in Romano-British period, 20; strip farming, 25, 28; in Domesday period, 28; rent for land, 29; poor

harvests, 30, 35, 92, 119; in 13th century, 33, 34; wool trade and sheep farming, 34, 36, 37, 41, 49, 53, 86, 92, 100; in 14th century, 35, 36; murrain, 35; sheep/corn agriculture, 37, 92, 100; in 16th century, 48, 49; in 17th century, 52, 53, 65; water meadows, 53; in 18th century, 68; in 19th century, 76, 77, 81, 85, 86, 89, 92; enclosure, 76, 85; Swing riots, 81, 86; repeal of the Corn Laws, 88; in the 20th century, 100, 101, 102, 104, 107, 116, 118, 119
Fennell, Joseph, 106
Fidler family, 105
Fisher, Pamela, 126
Fitz family, 67
Fitz Farm, 107
Fitz House, 104, 105, 110, 122, 123
Fitz, Richard, 55
Fitz, Walter, 55, 76, 85, 93
Foorsbroke, Elizabeth, 59
Ford, Henry, 89, 91
Ford, Jack, 81
Francis Frith Collection, 126
Freeman, Bert, 15
French, Colonel Charles, 105
Fulcher, Robert, 87
Gatty, Hester, 110
Geology: Carboniferous period, 6; Devonian period, 6; Permian period, 7; Triassic period, 7; Portland stone, 7, 8; Jurassic period, 7; Purbeck stone, 7, 8; fossils, 7; Cretaceous period, 7; Wealden stone, 7; Greensand stone, 8; gault clay, 8; chalk, 8; spring line, 8; flint, 8; Tertiary Age, 8; Ice Age, 9; Pleistocene period, 9
Giles, Charles, 107, 113, 119, 120, 124
Giles, Edith, 117
Giles, Julia, 114
Godfrey de Ewyas, 31, 32, 33
Godwin, 26
Goldens, 96, 105, 112, 117
Goodfellow family, 66
Goodfellow, Bill, 109, 110, 112, 116, 123
Goodfellow, Ely, 89
Goodfellow, George, 66
Goodfellow, Henry, 91
Goodfellow, John, 75
Goodfellow, Vic, 110
Grandison, William de, 36
Greystones, 126
Grovely Ridge, 16, 18, 22
Grovely Wood, 11, 14
Gunfrid Maldit, 27
Hanging Langford Camp, 16
Hardiman, Bill, 110, 112
Hardiman, Frank, 107
Harington, Sir James, 59
Harnett, Sydney, 94
Harold, King, 26
Harold, Lord of Sudely, Baron of Ewyas, 29, 30, 31
Harris, Edward, 89, 91
Haucks, Henry, 47, 48
Hayter, Augustus, 55, 65
Herbert, George, 11th Earl of Pembroke, 75, 85, 87
Herbert, Henry, 2nd Earl of Pembroke, 51
Herbert, Henry, 9th Earl of Pembroke, 67, 75
Herbert, Henry, 10th Earl of Pembroke, 69, 75
Herbert, Philip, 4th Earl of Pembroke, 53, 54, 57
Herbert, Philip, 5th Earl of Pembroke, 60, 61
Herbert, Philip, 7th Earl of Pembroke, 61
Herbert, Robert, 12th Earl of Pembroke, 87, 93
Herbert, Sydney, 87
Herbert, Thomas, 8th Earl of Pembroke, 67
Herbert, William, 1st Earl of Pembroke, 43, 44
Herbert, William, 3rd Earl of Pembroke, 51, 52
Herbert, William, 6th Earl of Pembroke, 61
Hewitt, John, 101
Hillside Cottages, 87
Hod Hill, 18
Hole in the Wall, 85, 93, 98
Holt Lane, 11
Holt Wood, 15
Home Close, 126
Home Farm, 65, 91, 106, 118, 125
Horrell, Ernest, 118
Horton family, 36
Howard, Henry Warwick, 106
Howards House, 56, 65, 82, 106, 122
Hungerford, Agnes, 42
Hungerford, Robert (Lord Molyns and Hungerford), 39
Hungerford, Robert, 39
Hungerford, Sir Edward, 42
Hungerford, Sir Edward, 54
Hungerford, Sir Thomas, 36, 37
Hungerford, Sir Walter II, 42, 43
Hungerford, Sir Walter, 40, 42
Hungerford, Thomas, 39
Hungerford, Walter, Lord, 38, 39
Hussey, Elizabeth, 42, 43
Hussey, Joan, 36, 37
Hussey, Reginald, 36
Jesse family, 62, 63, 67
John de Tregoze, 33
Johnson, Peter, 125
Jones, Inigo, 57
Jukes, George, 98
Jukes-Browne, A, 7
Karlo, 26, 28
Keatinge, Ellen, 97, 106

Keatinge, Gerald, 96, 97, 101, 105, 106, 111, 112, 113, 117
Keatinge, Kitty, 95, 117, 122
Keatinge, Richard, 97
Keatinge, Sir Edgar, 20, 56, 117, 118, 119, 120
Keatinge, Walter, 97
Keatinge-Clay, Paffard, 101, 109, 110, 125
Keatinge-Clay, Rev William, 109, 110
Keevil, John, 93
Kellow, Elizabeth, 99
Kellow, Job, 86, 89
Kellow, Thomas, 98
Knights Hospitallers, 34
Kynmerick, Johannes de, 36
Lancaster-Rankin, Major General and Margery, 121
Larkham family, 75, 76, 77, 98
Larkham's Farm, 77
Larkin, Jem, 81
Larkin, Lilian, 103
Lear, Frances, 78, 83, 88
Lee, Alice, 97, 101, 106, 111
Lee, Jack, 123
Lee, Robert, 97
Lever, Ron, 20, 119, 120
Ley Chapel, 39, 60, 66, 68, 88, 95
Ley Farm, 12, 106, 120, 125
Ley, Henry, 2nd Earl of Marlborough, 51
Ley, Henry, 39, 46, 47, 49, 50
Ley, James, 3rd Earl of Marlborough, 54, 55, 56, 57, 60
Ley, James, 50, 51
Ley, John, 50
Ley, Matthew, 50
Ley, William, 50
Lime kilns, 88, 100
Lockhart, Tom Ashe, 63
Long, John, 47
Lower Farm, 87
Ludlow, Captain, 56
Lush, John, 85
Macey family, 75, 76, 85, 91
Maiden Castle, 18
Malthouse (Bucks Close), 67, 85, 121
Manor Farm (Teffont Evias), 79, 88, 91, 94
Manor Farm (Teffont Magna), 60, 93, 98, 107, 118, 124, 125
Marlborough, Duke of, 66
Maudslay, Charles, and his sister, 96, 97, 101, 105
Mayhew, Henry, 47, 48
Mayne (de Salis), Emily, 87, 88, 89, 90, 91, 93, 94, 95, 96
Mayne, Augustus, 83
Mayne, Christopher, 63, 64, 66
Mayne, Elizabeth, 67, 68
Mayne, Isabella, 68
Mayne, John Jr, 67, 68
Mayne, John Thomas, 78, 79, 82, 83, 84, 87
Mayne, John, 67
Mayne, Margaret, 96
Mayne, Sarah, 78, 91
Mayne, Thomas Jr, 73, 75, 78
Mayne, Thomas, 68, 69
Mellowes, William, 48
Merley (lawyer), 96
Methodist Mission House/Chapel, 77, 103
Miles, Walter, 36
Mill Farm, 118, 121, 125
Mill, 87, 91, 96
Miller, Dr and Mrs Graham, 125
Mills, Thomas, 68
Mompesson family, 64, 66
Montague Cottage, 65
Moody, Mr, 73
Mordaunt-Hare, Major and Mrs, 122, 123
Mould family, 67, 76
Mullens (Daw), Grace, 69
Mullins, Thomas, 97
Nadder, River, 8, 9, 12, 16, 125, 128
Nairy, Cis, 116
Nepean, Lieutenant-Colonel Evan and Cicily, 121
Newall, R S, 15, 21, 120
Norman Conquest, 27
Norris, Richard, 85
Old Sarum, 22, 27
Old School House, 89
Olivier, Edith, 104, 110, 116
Orchards, 100
Osbern Pentecost, 28
Osmond, 24, 25
Parker, David, 126
Parnel de Ewyas, 33
Parsons, Virginia, 112
Pembroke Estate Survey of the Manors of Dinton and Teffont 1631-32, 52, 53, 67
Pembroke, Sir William, 47
Penny family, 118, 121
Penruddock, Colonel, 58
Philippa de Ewyas, 33
Phipp, John II, 60, 66
Phipp, John, 55, 57, 60
Piped water supply, 94
Pitcairn, Alastair and Angus, 124
Prehistory: Palaeolithic era, 9; flora and fauna, 9, 10; first appearance of man, 9; tools and artefacts, 9-21; Neanderthal man, 10; homo sapiens sapiens, 10; Mesolithic era, 10, 11; Neolithic era, 11, 12, 13; farming, 12, 16, 20; trade, 13, 16, 17; long barrows, 13, 24; round

barrows, 13, 14, 15; Bronze Age, 14, 15; Beaker People, 14, 15; the Amesbury Archer, 15; Iron Age, 16, 17; hill-forts, 16, 17, 18; Grims Ditch, 17; Iron Age burial, 17; coins, 17; Durotriges, 17, 18; Celts, 17; Romano-British era, 18, 19, 20, 21; Romano-British burials, 19, 20; Romano-British shrine/look-out post, 21
Quarries: Teffont, 7, 15, 19, 20, 65, 67, 88, 100, 120; Chilmark, 7, 15, 19, 34, 62, 67, 113; Tisbury, 34; Goldens, 42; Butts Hill, 100
Railway, Salisbury-Yeovil, 88
Rawlins, John, 60
Rectory (Bridges), 65, 82, 122, 123
Robert de Tregoze, 33
Robert of Ewyas, 31
Romans: trade with, 17; coins, 17, 21; Claudian invasion, 18; presence in Teffont area, 19; villas, 19; hypocausts, 21; departure from Britain, 21
Rowden, John, 48
Rowden, William, 66
Salis, William Fane de, 90
Salisbury Cathedral, 7, 34
Sassoon, Siegfried, 110
Saxon cross, 24, 25, 30, 55
Saxons: invasions, 22; settlement, 22; artefacts, 24; burials, 24, 25
Scammell, Frank, 88
Schools: set up by Emily Mayne, 89; in Teffont Magna, 89; church school, Dinton, 89; Dinton Elementary School, 92; Teffont Magna Elementary School, 92, 111
Scott, George Gilbert, 81, 82
Scott, Rev Sir Douglas, 101, 102
Seagrim, William, 77
Shaftesbury Abbey, 25, 26, 27, 32, 36, 41, 42, 43, 44
Shaw, Colonel Kennedy, 107, 110, 113, 118, 120
Shergold, John, 89
Shergold, Mary Ann, 77, 89
Sigestan, 25
Skelton, Paul, 125
Smith, Oliver, 70, 76
Somerset, Duke of, 43
South Cadbury, 22
Spencer, Fred, 118
Spring, 8, 17, 19, 94, 128
Squarey, Elias, 87
St Edward, 26
St Edward's church, 26
St Maur, Dionysia de, 46, 83
St Peter's Abbey, Gloucester, 31
Stained glass, Dutch medieval, 82
Stapledon, Sir George, 116
Stapleford, 9
Start, John, 88
Start, Mary Anna, 78
Stockton Earthworks, 17
Stonehenge, 12, 13, 15, 16
Sutton, Mr and Mrs, 96
Swallowcliffe Down, 24, 25
Swindon, 22
Sydney, Sir Philip, 51
Teffont place-name meaning, 19, 22
Teffont Reading Room, 103
Teffont stream, 8, 94, 109, 128
Tennant, David, 111, 112
Tennant, Stephen, 110
Thatcher family, 125
Thatcher, John, 120
Thickthorn Copse, 11
Tisbury, 8, 33, 38, 41
Triqueti, Henri de, 95
Trotter, Alexander and Alys, 103, 111, 122
Turnpike road, 69, 77
Upper Holt, 21
Vikings, 24, 25
Vineyard, 60, 126
Vining, John and Julia (Crossman), 124, 125
Walker, Mr and Mrs Kenneth, 106
Walton, William, 110
Ward, Samuel Broomshead, 82, 88, 91, 92
Wardour Castle, 54, 55
Waterman, Jonathan, 68
Webb, John (architect), 57
Webb, John, 125
Whistler, Rex and Laurence, 110
White, Edmund, 81
Wick Ball Camp, 16
Wilde, Brian, 125
Willan, Brigadier Hugh, 122, 123
Willan, Group-Captain Andrew and Joan, 123
Wilton House, 49, 51, 57, 67, 75
Wilton, 22, 25, 31
Women's Institute history of Teffont, 121
Woodlands, Teffont Evias, 97, 106, 117, 119
World War I casualties, 102, 103
World War II casualties, 119
Wrens Cottage, 115, 126
Wyatt, James, 75
Wylye valley, 16, 22, 53
Wyndham, Ella, 83, 89
Wyndham, William, 66, 75, 78, 81, 82, 83, 93

SUBSCRIBERS

H D Adlard
M Andrews
Ann Ashton
Barbara Baker
Richard and Lucie Barlow Pool
Sheila Barr
Sarah and Matthew Bell
Professor and Mrs Alastair Bellingham
Dr Karen Blake
Michael and Anne Bolwell
Lt Col and Mrs Robin Bridges
Mrs Margaret Briggs
Jill Brown
Jason Buck, Sebastian Buck
John Buck and Isobel Hall
Richard and Ruth Bull
Maurice and Jean Busbridge
Kate and Paul Busbridge
Geoffrey, Lynn, Livvy, George and Sophie Button
Andrew and Rose Chapman
Marjorie Coleman
Mr and Mrs Jonathan Croft
James Crouch
William and Cherida Daniel
Ian and Jackie Dawson
Elizabeth and Peter Dawson
Mary Corrie and Tony Deane
Alan and Margaret Dodge, Freshford
The Rev John and Dr Ruth Eade
Jake, Louise and Rufus Eastham
Michael Faramus
Robin and Zillah Faulkner
Ele Fisher, Jonty Fisher
John and Pamela Fisher
Joan and Jonathan Foster
David and Margaret Foy
Mr Bert Freeman
Betty and Ronald Gerelli
Lesley and Ruth Gill
Priscilla Gillingham
Dr and Mrs T M D Gimlette
Elizabeth and Bill Goodfellow
Georgie and Tallula Green
Mrs Betty Gregory
Bill Hardiman
Richard Hawkins and Carol Jacobs
Violet Hoare
Hugh and Fiona Homan
Howards House Hotel
Diana Jefford
Harold and Jean Johnston
Ron and Heather Kann
Mary Keatinge, Dr Richard Keatinge
Professor William Keatinge
Peggy Kellow
Ben Kerwood
Victoria Knowles
Sarah Larkham
Alice Lee
Felicity Little
Thomas Ashe Lockhart
Richard andPaddy Long-Fox
Mr and Mrs J K Lowry
Vanessa and Graham McCracken
Richard, Pat and Keri McNamara
Mr and Mrs Philip Medcalf
Mrs Marcelle Membrey
Dr Graham Miller
Paolo and Fields Miurin
Bob and Wanda Moffat
Major T R Mordaunt-Hare and Carolyn Troup
Sir Evan and Lady Nepean
Jenny and Nick de B Nicholson
Dr Kenneth and Mrs Susan Nicoll
Major G O'Hara MBE and Mrs M O'Hara
Joan Parsons
G Penny
Agnes and Cecily Perry Robinson
Ralph and Amanda Perry Robinson
Alison and Jane Pitcairn
Don and Anita Ridley
Joan Rowden
Bryan and Evelyne Sarginson
Lord and Lady Sharman
Norman and Jane Stevens
Georgina and David Stocks
Mr and Mrs Barrie Symons
Sarah Owen and Barry Taylor
Tony and Jill Thomas
Sue Tyler
Antoinette and Peter Wacher
Edward and Antonia Waddinton
Joan Welland
Sir David and Lady West Ressell
Mr and Mrs Ernest Whitby
Geoffrey and Mary Whitby
Brian and Sarah Wilde
Richard and Sarah Willan
Tim and Ann Woolley